Be With Me

Fedd Books
P.O. Box 341973
Austin, TX 78734
www.thefeddagency.com

Published in association with The Fedd Agency, Inc., a literary agency.

ISBN: 978-1-949784-66-4
eISBN: 978-1-949784-67-1

Library of Congress Control Number: 2021906059

Printed in the United States of America

First Edition 15 14 13 12 11 / 10 9 8 7 6 5 4 3 2

To God's children

Contents

I want you to know how much I treasure you!
I want you to know how proud I am of you!
I want you to know how special you are to Me!
I want you to know how beautiful you are to Me!
I love you completely, sweet child!

Preface

Love.

Something that everyone craves.

Something that everyone needs.

Something that everyone searches for.

Theoretically, finding love seems so simple. We see it in movies. We read it in books. We watch those around us find it and make it last. Yet sometimes finding love for ourselves can seem so difficult.

How do we obtain real love—lasting love—the ultimate love?

After I graduated from college, I decided that I was going to take on the world. I was going to have it all—an amazing husband, three children, and a successful career. And, of course, I was going to have *love*.

Only that didn't happen. Instead, I have been divorced two times. I have one child and am now (happily) married for the third time. How did that happen? It obviously took me some time to get here, but I've learned a few things. First, I have learned that God is the only source of love that fully satisfies. Second, I have learned that we need to have God at the center of our lives. We need to have a close, personal relationship with Him. We need to ask Him to guide us in all the choices that we make.

While all of our stories are different, we all experience the storms of life—the storms that come crashing in without warning. But storms do have their upside. How we handle our storms, how we react to our storms, and how we learn from our storms shape who we are and who we will become. However, to get through the storms and come out on the other side, we must understand that our only refuge is in God and God alone.

Fortunately, I was raised with God in my life. My family went to church every Sunday, and we often prayed together. So when my life began to fall apart, I knew that God was the answer. What I did not know was how He would rescue me.

I used to say, *God—just come down here and tell me what to do!* But that never happened. Then one day I attended a seminar about learning to hear God's voice through a contemplative journaling program. After my experience there, my life would forever be changed. There I learned that I could actually have God lead my life!

It is these experiences, the lessons that God has taught me, and more, that I want to share with you. I want to share with you how much God truly loves us and desires for us to allow Him to be the center of our lives. When that happens, our lives can be truly glorious!

STORMS

To give you more context regarding my journey to find love, I want to tell you about a few significant milestones I've encountered along the way.

I was married for seventeen years to my first husband, the best result of which is my beautiful daughter, who is now grown. We had fun while dating, but we were very far apart on many of the important aspects of marriage and life. We had different viewpoints on God, relationships, family, children, money, careers, and so much more. After having my daughter at the age of twenty-seven, the depths of these differences created an impassable gap between us.

After almost two decades together, we decided to divorce. This decision was not taken lightly. I believe that marriage is a sacred and holy commitment between two people made before God. Our relationship, though, had cracked, splintered, and was broken. There was no putting the pieces back together.

Then came marriage number two. You always hear about rebound relationships. I not only had one of my own, but I decided to marry my rebound. This proved to be disastrous. I could not have found someone more opposite to my ethics and morals.

My rebound husband chose to move out of our home one day while I was at work. This came as a complete surprise to me. Sure, we had had some difficulties, but I was always under the impression that we could work things out. I had been divorced before and was mortified at the idea of going down that path again. But in the end, he left.

The resulting pain to both my daughter and me was astronomical, but looking back, I see that I needed to reach that point of complete brokenness in order to fully submit to God.

I slipped into a depression. I was still working and raising my child, but I became a shell of the person I was. I was a ghost, just going through the motions. I felt like such a failure.

But once again, the faith of my childhood reminded me that I needed to pray to God for help. Finally one day, in a fit of crying, I looked up to God and told Him that I could no longer do this.

I surrendered my life to Him, knowing that only He could fix the mess I had made of my life. At that very moment, I felt a calmness and tingling wash over me from my head to my toes. I have since learned that what I did that day was to surrender to God. I literally felt Him take the burden off my shoulders. I knew at that moment that I was going to survive—and more than that, I was going to be okay.

After my surrender, God led me through a series of events that changed my life forever. God put people in my life who taught me that I could have a closer relationship with Him—that a relationship with God could be more than just going to church. I attended a retreat through an organization called One Simple Voice. Once there, I knew I was home. What I learned there was the answer to many of my struggles in life. An answer to calming the storms. Of course, that answer was a personal relationship with God.

My time there taught me that I could hear God through a contemplative journaling program. I dove in wholeheartedly. I began to journal daily, many times waking up before the sun came up. I so desperately wanted to hear God. I wanted Him to guide my life. Who better to help me than the One who knows me best and who loves me most?

How did my journaling journey change my life? How long did it take for me to hear God? How did I begin to learn so many lessons? I didn't hear God's voice right away. In fact, it took me seventy days. Seventy! Seventy days of journaling, asking, and waiting.

I officially started to journal on July 12, 2012. For fifty-seven days straight I continued to ask the question, *God, are You there?* Finally, on day fifty-seven, a hummingbird flew up to the window and looked directly at me. I was so elated because I had no doubt that God had sent me that hummingbird.

During the next few weeks, I began to see signs that God was there, but I was still not "empty" enough to hear Him. I had signs from nature (butterflies, dragonflies, and birds) and elsewhere—wind chimes would sound without the wind, bushes would rustle without a breeze, and much more.

Then, on August 3, 2012, day seventy of my journaling journey, I finally heard God's voice. My conversation that day went like this: *God, are You there?* I started to cry. I just wept. *God, how did my life turn out this way? God, please tell me You are here. I have to know that You're here.*

And then I heard it. I heard God's voice: "Calm down. I am. It's okay."

I said, *I don't want to be alone.*

I then heard, "You are not alone. I am here."

My Savior, my God, spoke to me and told me that I was not alone and that I was going to be okay. My sobs turned to joy. God has always answered me with such kind and loving words. The beautiful relationship with God that has formed since I started hearing Him has changed my life. I finally found that love I was searching for. God had been with me all along.

Do I still have storms in my life? Of course I do, but these storms seem less severe when I walk through them with God. As the days and months and years have gone by, the lessons that God has taught me have become longer and more in-depth. I am full of questions, and He is full of answers. I have asked Him about love, forgiveness, faith, surrender, truth, stress, struggles—and the list goes on. I am excited to share with you what I have learned. I hope you see the incredible love that God has for you. May God bless you, and may this book fill you with His love.

CHAPTER 1

Love

Love is the nutrient needed to survive. Me and Love—words that can be interchanged.

God is love. It's that simple. If you are wondering where to start on your journey to love, know that God has already told us. All He wants is for us to love each other. How do we do this as humans? So much gets in the way—we get in the way. But God has taught me that everyone needs love and that love is the foundation of life. He has also taught me how important it is to love our spouse, children, and neighbor fully and selflessly. In fact, the Bible tells us that God's two greatest commandments are all about love—loving God and loving others.

Day 1

Love is the foundation of Me and of life, for without love, you have hell. This is because when there is no love, there is no Me. I am synonymous with love. Love equals Me. A home of love is so beautiful because love is the foundation. Love is like concrete. It is strong and able to hold up a house. However, a house built on sand will wash away because there is not a foundation of love, of concrete. Many houses look beautiful on the outside, but they are unstable because of the lack of love—the lack of Me. The foundation is shaky or shifting. The people in the home cannot figure out why the home is unstable. It is the lack of Me. Bring Me into the home and the foundation is shored up; it is strengthened, and the house becomes stable. If you do not bring Me in, the home will continue to crumble, just as your life crumbles and breaks apart when I am not there. Bring Me in and your life becomes a pillar of strength. You may be breaking to the point of crumbling, but if you surrender to Me and open the door to let Me in, you will be able to stop the crumbling and strengthen your foundation. You will become fortified. Then you can strengthen your life, you can become a pillar, and your home will become a place of strength with Me.

> *"Love the Lord your God with all your heart and with all your soul and with all your mind and with all your strength." The second is this: "Love your neighbor as yourself." There is no commandment greater than these.*
> (Mark 12:30–31 NIV)

If loving God and loving others is the best foundation to build our homes on, how likely or unlikely is yours to be swept away by a storm? Reflect on your response.

Day 2

Love one another. That is so easy and yet so difficult. Love is My foundation. Love is the foundation of Christianity, but so often you forget that. You get so tied up in all the traditions that you forget about love. You can never go wrong if you just love. Love your neighbor as yourself, and love Me. When you do this, everything falls into place.

> *Do everything in love.*
> (1 Corinthians 16:14 NIV)

How can you get better at loving your neighbor as yourself?

Day 3

Humans make love difficult and complicated. It is so easy. Love each other. If you are not loving each other, then you are not doing My will. Loving one another is one way to love Me. Know that everyone is My child and I love them, so you should love them too. It sounds easy, but I understand how hard it is. Society today makes it difficult. Do not be judgmental of one another. When you are not being judgmental, it is so much easier to love one another.

> *Do not judge, or you too will be judged.*
> (Matthew 7:1 NIV)

Does being judgmental of others hinder your love?

Day 4

Be loving. Remember, this is the key to life. The key is love. When you practice love at all times, you will find that life is easier. Life is more fulfilling. When you show love to others, you can change their life. Everyone needs to have love in their life. So be love. Be My instrument. When in doubt on what to do, just be love.

> *Whoever does not love does not know God,*
> *because God is love.* (1 John 4:8 NIV)

How has receiving love changed your life? How could you give love to change someone else's life?

Day 5

Continue to keep Me at the center of your life, and most importantly, continue to be love, for I am love. Love is a reflection of Me. Love shows others Me in you. Love is the most basic thing, yet it is the most important thing in the world and in life because love is Me. When I am your primary focus, it is much easier for you to show love to others.

> *And so we know and rely on the love God has for us. God is love. Whoever lives in love lives in God, and God in them.* (1 John 4:16 NIV)

Do you know that when you show love to others, you are reflecting God within you?

Day 6

Love is at the center of every human being. Love is the center of life. Lack of love or love being covered up is the center of evil. The absence of love is at the center of hate, anger, guilt, and all the negatives in life. Love is the basic bread of life because love equals Me, and I am the Bread of Life. So love gives life.

> *The bread of God is the bread that comes down from heaven. He gives life to the world.*
> (John 6:33)

Now that you know that God is love and is at the center of your life, take it one step further. Love is at the center of every human being. Reflect upon the fact that everyone you come in contact with has love at their center. Now reflect upon those whom you do not see as love, realizing that they do have love at their center, but it is just covered up. How, then, will you respond differently to them now?

Day 7

Love is the ultimate commandment. Love Me and love your neighbor. That is pretty simple. Does it say to love yourself? No, but that is what has happened with society. You have gotten away from putting Me and your neighbor first and have instead put yourself first. This creates all sorts of havoc. People begin making choices to benefit themselves instead of Me and their neighbor. This leads to all kinds of evil, such as greed, love of money, hate, and lust. When you make the choice for Me and your neighbor, there is love. Love leads to kindness, patience, and generosity—all good things. When you choose Me and your neighbor, peacefulness of the heart prevails. Life is not difficult when people choose love. If everyone would just love Me and their neighbor, life would be so much more peaceful and glorious. You get a glimpse of heaven on Earth when you experience such love.

> *Most of all, love one another deeply. Love erases many sins by forgiving them.* (1 Peter 4:8)

What are a few ways that you can choose God and others over yourself today?

Day 8

There are many types of love, but My love is the greatest. My love for you is greater than the love between a man and a woman. It is even greater than the love a mother has for her child. You are unable to comprehend the amount of love that I have for you. This is why it is so upsetting to Me when My children turn from Me. Imagine your child or spouse turning away from you. How much would that hurt? When My children turn away from Me, it hurts even more than that. But when a child returns to Me, the joy I feel is endless. As in the story of the prodigal son, I will always forgive My children when they ask for forgiveness because My love is beyond measure.

> *While the son was still a long way off, his father saw him. He was filled with tender love for his son. He ran to him. He threw his arms around him and kissed him.* (Luke 15:20)

Did you know that God is hurt and saddened when you turn from Him? How does knowing that make you feel?

Day 9

Your love for others in your life pales in comparison to My love for you. I love you even more than you can imagine. Humans cannot fathom the depth of My love. I love each and every one of you. There is nothing that can separate you from My love.

> *I am absolutely sure that not even death or life can separate us from God's love. Not even angels or demons, the present or the future, or any powers can separate us.* (Romans 8:38)

Have you ever thought about the depth of God's love for you and that nothing can separate you from His love?

Day 10

Know that I am the only one who can love you fully. I love you fully for you and for who you are. I fully know, accept, and love you. I am the only one whose love never wavers, never fades, and remains unaffected by your actions. My love for you is so deep and wide that it cannot be described but only experienced. Will you allow Me to love you?

> *Not even the highest places or the lowest, or anything else in all creation can separate us. Nothing at all can ever separate us from God's love. That's because of what Christ Jesus our Lord has done.* (Romans 8:39)

God knows all of your inner thoughts, actions, mistakes, and indiscretions, yet He still loves you fully. How does this make you feel?

Day 11

I created all of My children for love, and when they are not of love, they become lost. They become lost in violence, greed, selfishness, hate, and other negative things. But when they are living with love, there is compassion, kindness, understanding, patience, and joy—positive things in life. Being love is truly simple, but it can be so difficult in the world today. So be a child of love, of Me, and experience the joys of life!

> *Love must be honest and true. Hate what is evil. Hold on to what is good.* (Romans 12:9)

When you choose to live a life of love, how will your life be different? How will your relationships be different with family, friends, and coworkers?

Day 12

Finding the right man or woman to partner with you in life can be difficult. Many people do not take it seriously. While you are on Earth, you might be given a spouse to help you raise children, to help you through difficult times, and to help you enjoy life. What has happened in the "me" society, though, is that people are depending on their spouses to make them happy. This is a disaster. You need to be happy with Me at the center of your life before you are healthy and can be happy with a spouse. So when finding a spouse, you need to make sure that you are God-centered first. Then find someone who is also in that same place.

> *Seek first his kingdom and his righteousness,*
> *and all these things will be given to you as well.*
> (Matthew 6:33 NIV)

If you are married, are you depending on your spouse for your happiness?

If you are single, are you God-centered in your own life while being patient to find a God-centered spouse?

Day 13

Let's discuss love in a relationship. When two people meet, there is a chemistry—a chemistry that makes them want to be together all of the time. Eventually, this chemistry fades, and they need to make a decision to stay together and love one another forever. The problem arises when a couple gets married, the chemistry fades, and they decide not to make the commitment to love each other forever—and then divorce happens. It is important that people understand the difference between chemistry and love before making a commitment to marriage.

> *[Love] always protects. It always trusts. It always hopes. It never gives up.* (1 Corinthians 13:7)

Do you understand the difference between chemistry and the commitment to love?

Day 14

I did not create you to be alone. You are social beings, and I created you with a longing for companionship, whether it be a spouse, family or friends. Society has gotten away from monogamous relationships. It has become acceptable not to be faithful to your spouse. I am not happy about this. That is why I addressed adultery in the Commandments. When you chose the one to be with, you made a commitment "for better or for worse" to be with that person for life. Choosing that person was your choice. Trust may be broken in unfaithfulness. Remember that society and hardness of heart contribute to unfaithfulness, and especially contributing to unfaithfulness is a lack of Me in the center of the lives of those who are married. I see this too often. I need to be brought back into the marriage. I need to be the center of your lives. This will help to stop unfaithfulness and the acceptance of this behavior in society.

> *The LORD God said, "It is not good for the man to be alone. I will make a helper who is just right for him."* (Genesis 2:18)

Do you feel that society has gotten in the way of a faithful marriage? If so, how?

Day 15

Children are the greatest gifts that I give, but they are on loan to you. I am allowing people to raise My children. Many parents do a great job, but there are others who are facing difficulties in their lives, and unfortunately this reflects in their parenting. It saddens Me when this happens to My greatest gift. Always remember that poor parenting is not the child's fault. These children will grow up to be adults, many of them with problems. Remember when you come in contact with difficult adults that many times, they are how they are as a result of their upbringing. You never know a person's full story. Just treat everyone you come in contact with as My child. Show patience and love to those who are difficult. Showing them love may be the difference in their lives that they need to change. Let them see Me in you.

> *Fathers, don't make your children bitter. If you do, they will lose hope.* (Colossians 3:21)

When meeting a difficult child or adult, can you remember that the way they are may be the result of their environment? Do you treat them with disdain or with love? Can you now react differently when you meet someone difficult?

Day 16

Love. It is like the root of a tree. A tree cannot grow without roots. A small tree developing roots cannot get bigger without its roots growing and expanding. The larger the root base is, the larger a tree can grow. A tree quickly grows and drops seeds to make more roots and more trees, and then there is an arbor. But none of this can happen without the first roots of the first tree. Without love, there is no tree, no seeds, and no arbors. But it just takes one tree. Show love and your tree will grow and prosper. Water? Yes, you need water. That is Me. When you become dry, I will help to water you. Soon your love will foster other love, and this will continue until there is an arbor of love. Remember, though, that all of this starts with just one person showing love, being love. It is My foundation. Love is the root of everything good, so be love. Sometimes you do not see the result of your love, for your roots are growing underground or a seed is sprouting for another tree. Do not ever doubt that your love is nourishing just because you do not see it.

> *But I am like a healthy olive tree.*
> *My roots are deep in the house of God.*
> *I trust in your faithful love*
> *for ever and ever.* (Psalm 52:8)

How can you spread your roots of love to those you do not know? Do you need to increase the water/God in your life? How can you do this?

Day 17

Love is so important. When you show love, even to strangers, it is contagious. When you are around your friends, show love. When you are around strangers, show love. When people see love in you, they see Me. Some don't realize that they are seeing love. They just want to be around it. There is a pull toward someone who shows love. Ultimately, that is Me. Often, showing love to someone can change their day, even their life. You may never know the impact you have on someone when you show them love. So just be loving. This is part of letting them see Me in you.

> *If you love one another, everyone will know you are my disciples.* (John 13:35)

Do others see God in you by the love you show them?

Day 18

Be a good steward of My love. I have given you an endless, immeasurable, unchanging love. Even if you gave a portion of that away, it still has the potential to change the world. Show people Me in you. Be loving. That is all I ask of My children. Be patient, be kind, and love everyone you come in contact with. When you show love to everyone, that is when you are most like Jesus. *Love* is a very powerful word, a very powerful emotion, and a very powerful action. Be loving. Show love. Be love.

> *I give you a new command. Love one another. You must love one another, just as I have loved you.* (John 13:34)

Are you a steward of God's love?

Day 19

Love is very powerful. Everyone, in their own way, is looking for love. People need to have love to survive. If people do not have love, they will die—either literally or figuratively. By showing love to people, you are making a difference in their lives, and you are showing them Me. You are showing them what is most important in life. This is why it is My greatest commandment.

> *The three most important things to have are faith, hope and love. But the greatest of them is love.*
> (1 Corinthians 13:13)

For one week, can you show love to everyone you come in contact with? How will you do this? Take note of their reaction and see the change in their disposition.

Day 20

Love your neighbor. This, as well as the first commandment, is taking a back seat in today's society. Many people are more concerned with themselves than with Me or their neighbor. All you can do is be the change you wish to see. Be kind to everyone you meet. Be loving, be generous, and be supportive. Do your best to be nonjudgmental. Many people are able to put Me first but struggle putting others first. Understand that putting others first *is* putting Me first.

> *None of you should look out just for your own good. Each of you should also look out for the good of others.* (Philippians 2:4)

Why do you think it is easier for modern-day Christians to put God first but not to put others first?

Day 21

Let's discuss love. Jesus showed His love, even to those who beat and tortured Him. How truly difficult it is to love those who have wronged you! How easy it is to love those who love you! Then there are those who are in the middle. They have not wronged you, but they are not in your circle of friends and family. How easy is it to love them? Keep an eye out for them. Many of them desperately need love—love from anyone.

> *Suppose you love those who love you. Should anyone praise you for that? Even sinners love those who love them.* (Luke 6:32)

How do you treat those in the "middle" of your life? Do you love them? What can you do differently to show love to those who are not in your inner circle?

Day 22

It all begins with love. When you are love and treat others with love, everything else falls into place. Think about it. Relationships equal love. When you truly are love, then you will have fewer issues in your life; but when you are not love, and you act with your ego, problems will prevail. Problems are caused by your ego. They are only solved by love. When you are all love, the ego cannot fit—it cannot be. Unfortunately, though, there are egos. How strong your ego is directly relates to how much difficulty you will have in relationships. If the ego always overpowers love, then you will encounter many problems. However, when you learn to squash the ego, you will have fewer problems. Life can be much easier and have fewer problems if you squash the ego and live by love.

> *Agree with one another. Don't be proud. Be willing to be a friend of people who aren't considered important. Don't think that you are better than others.* (Romans 12:16)

What is at least one relationship in which your ego needs to decrease and your love needs to increase?

Day 23

You know that love is My foundation, for if you are of love, you are of Me. If you are not love, you are not of Me. At birth, everyone is love. Everyone is My child, My love. Over time, though, many people stop being of love when they become consumed by their egos. They lose sight of what love truly is. This is very sad. The heart has become so covered by the ego that the soul is smothered and cannot breathe. The ego has taken over. The ego is not of love. So when I say you are not of love, I am speaking of the ego. The ego is not of Me. It is a product of society, of self-centeredness, and of evil. But the ego will die at death, and all that will remain is the soul. The soul is able to breathe again, and the ego lies next to the soul—crumbled and full of death.

> *Dear friends, let us love one another, because love comes from God. Everyone who loves has become a child of God and knows God. Anyone who does not love does not know God, because God is love.*
> (1 John 4:7–8)

Have you allowed your soul to be covered by your ego? How can you break down your ego and return to love?

Day 24

So many people put parameters and conditions on love. Many people use love as a weapon, but love is pure and kind. True love has no parameters or conditions. That is My love for you. That is My love for all of My children. Pure love. So many people are afraid of losing love because of what they have done. I will never love My children any less because of their actions. Will I be disappointed or have great sadness? Yes, but My love will never diminish. Love is not to be used as a means of manipulation, yet many use it that way. This saddens Me greatly. Many people attribute love to only doing what someone wants, and if they do not do it, they will lose love. My love for you is pure love, and I want you to give others pure love.

> *There is no fear in love. Instead, perfect love drives away fear. That's because fear has to do with being punished. The one who fears does not have perfect love.* (1 John 4:18)

What are some parameters or conditions that you have put on love?

Day 25

My wish for all humanity is that there would be love and kindness everywhere, that people would truly care about and love their neighbors, that people would treat others with love, and that hate would be abolished.

> *The light shines in the darkness. But the darkness has not overcome the light.* (John 1:5)

How can you bring the light of Christ (love) into the darkness (absence of love)?

Day 26

Jesus was the ultimate example of showing love for one's neighbor. Ultimate love was shown the day He carried His own cross up the hill and laid down His life for you. Even during all of this, He did not lash out at anyone—because He knew they had no idea what they were actually doing. Instead of hate, He showed love. This is so difficult for My children to do. Love your neighbor—even those who are destructive to you.

> *Jesus said, "Father, forgive them. They don't know what they are doing."* (Luke 23:34)

Does knowing that those who are destructive to you *don't know what they are doing* help you to love them?

Day 27

Just remember that love will always prevail—in everything and in every situation. The pendulum will swing back to love. It always does, from large issues such as war, to smaller issues such as relationships. It always swings back. Evil will not like it, but evil will never win!

> *I have told you these things, so that you can have peace because of me. In this world you will have trouble. But be encouraged! I have won the battle over the world.* (John 13:33)

Do you feel as if the pendulum in your life has swung away from love? What can you do to help it swing back?

CHAPTER 2

Forgiveness

Forgiveness is the ultimate path to peacefulness and freedom.

To forgive is one of the toughest things for us to do. When we feel wronged, many of us immediately go to our egos instead of our hearts. If we were always in our hearts, where God resides, we would be able to forgive immediately—but we often enjoy playing the victim. Sometimes being a victim can even become our identity. So what should we do? We should ask God to help us forgive. He has taught me that the burden of carrying unforgiveness becomes extremely heavy and keeps us from having peace and joy in our lives. I have also learned that forgiving others is not only for the person we are forgiving, but it is also for ourselves. By forgiving, we free ourselves up for the happiness life can bring. Most importantly, we create space for God.

Day 28

I will always forgive My children. All that is needed is for My children to ask for forgiveness and genuinely mean it. If one asks but is not repentant, there is no forgiveness. Think about forgiveness with your children. You will always forgive them. "I'm sorry" are some of the most powerful words, two of the most beautiful words, in the human language. It is beautiful when someone says "I'm sorry" to you and means it. This is only step one. Step two is forgiveness. Forgiveness can actually be more difficult, but to offer forgiveness is one of the most powerful, life-giving things you can do.

> *But they make themselves humble in my sight. They pray and look to me. And they turn from their evil ways. Then I will listen to them from heaven. I will forgive their sin. And I will heal their land. After all, they are my people.*
> (2 Chronicles 7:14)

Have you ever asked for forgiveness but were not repentant? What is the difference?

Day 29

Always keep in mind that a person who wrongs you usually does not do it intentionally. They do not purposefully set out to hurt you. The ability to forgive someone when they do not say they are sorry is truly beautiful. That is true love. That is My love.

> *Forgive other people when they sin against you. If you do, your Father who is in heaven will also forgive you.* (Matthew 6:14)

When others hurt you, do you realize that they usually do not do so on purpose? Do you forgive those who hurt you?

Day 30

I always forgive My children, for I am able to see into their hearts. I know if they are truly sorry when they ask for forgiveness. Only I know. Humans are unable to know this. That is why you need to ask one another for forgiveness. You need to give forgiveness regardless of whether or not someone asks you. This is very difficult, but this is carrying out the commandment of loving your neighbor as yourself. Forgiveness stems from love. When you forgive, you also receive healing. When you harbor hate for someone and do not forgive them, you are also hurting yourself. Forgiving someone shows love for the one you forgive, and it also benefits you and your healing.

> *Be kind and compassionate to one another, forgiving each other, just as in Christ God forgave you.* (Ephesians 4:32 NIV)

Have you ever forgiven someone who did not ask for forgiveness? How did that make you feel?

Day 31

Hate and hurt blind us from reality, but it is always a choice to forgive. Forgiveness cleanses the soul for both people—for the person who is being forgiven and for the person who is doing the forgiving. Forgiveness allows you and the person you forgive to heal.

> *May the Lord make your love increase and overflow for each other and for everyone else, just as ours does for you.* (1 Thessalonians 3:12 NIV)

Are there people from whom you have withheld your forgiveness? Are you willing to work toward forgiveness?

Day 32

Forgiveness and loving those who have wronged you can be very difficult. When you have been hurt, especially when you have been hurt deeply, it is very difficult to love the person who hurt you. Sometimes forgiveness takes time and is a process. I ask that you forgive those who have trespassed against you. Sometimes you may need to forgive many times. Remember—I have forgiven you many times.

> *Peter came to Jesus. He asked, "Lord, how many times should I forgive my brother or sister who sins against me? Up to seven times?" Jesus answered, "I tell you, not seven times, but 77 times." (Matthew 18:21–22)*

Is there someone you need to forgive—again?

Day 33

When someone hurts you badly, forgiveness is difficult. Much of this difficulty is because of your mind. When you keep replaying things that have happened, your mind is telling you not to forgive. As I have said, *"Forgiveness comes from your heart."* Your heart wants to forgive, but your mind does not want to forgive. Put forgiveness in your heart where I am. I will help you to forgive and to love.

> *He doesn't punish us for our sins as much as we should be punished.*
> *He doesn't pay us back in keeping with the evil things we've done.*
> *He loves those who have respect for him.*
> *His love is as high as the heavens are above the earth.* (Psalm 103:10–11)

Do you find yourself replaying the transgressions of others? Does this make it difficult to forgive?

Day 34

Sometimes it is tough to break down your ego to get to forgiveness. You know you have experienced this. The ego can be your biggest stumbling block. Put forgiveness in the heart when you start to think about the things a person has done; otherwise, the unforgiveness may become your identity. Surrender your ego to Me. Surrender your pain to Me. No longer worry about it. Put it in the past. Let Me be your identity. If you do this, you have forgiveness. If the situation comes up by others in a conversation, just let it go. Surrender it back to Me. Just tell the person, "It is in my past, and I have forgiven. I do not want my identity tied to that situation anymore." This will be tough because you might want the attention. Your ego wants to be a victim. Release it, surrender it, and humble yourself. You will feel at peace. Give complete forgiveness. Try it, make it a habit, and it will work.

> *Be humble in front of the Lord. And he will lift you up.* (James 4:10)

Do you like to dwell on a situation in which you feel you have been wronged, or are you able to forgive and move on?

Day 35

The topic of forgiveness is very important for My children. Remember—the word "forgiveness" is very easy. You know intellectually that you need to forgive, and in your heart you know that you need to forgive, but it can be very difficult to do. Your ego does not want you to forgive because not forgiving gives your ego identity. *I was wronged, I'm a victim, I'm angry, I'm suffering*—all of this negativity. However, when you surrender to Me, I will melt away all of this negativity, and I will help you to forgive. By doing so, you are able to heal, and you are able to have peace in your heart.

> *There is joy for those who work to bring peace.*
> (Proverbs 12:20)

What is holding you back from offering full forgiveness to someone right now?

Day 36

When you forgive, a weight is lifted off your shoulders. It feels wonderful because through forgiveness, you are able to heal. It is the most important step in healing. Unforgiveness can become part of your identity. Your ego loves being the victim, but if you were to forgive, you would be set free. Forgiveness is very liberating, and it brings you peace. Once you forgive, you are no longer bound to your past but can embrace wholeness and healing. It is very easy to get caught up in being a victim. Your ego takes over, but that victimization will cover your heart. When you get rid of that, through forgiveness, you are free and your heart shines through. How beautiful!

> *Brothers and sisters, I don't consider that I have taken hold of it yet. But here is the one thing I do. I forget what is behind me. I push hard toward what is ahead of me.* (Philippians 3:13)

Why do you hold on to unforgiveness? Can you see the damage of holding on to the past?

Day 37

Unforgiveness comes between you and Me. It takes up our space together. Look at all the time a smoker spends smoking. What a waste of time hurting yourself! It is the same with being unforgiving. That wastes so much time that you and I could be together in joy and peace. Which do you want to choose? Do you want to choose Me and our time together, or will you choose unforgiveness, anger, and even hate? Life is too short to concern yourself with unforgiveness; choose peace, love, and joy—and more importantly, choose us!

> *Do not judge, and you will not be judged. Do not condemn, and you will not be condemned. Forgive, and you will be forgiven.* (Luke 6:37 NIV)

What would choosing peace, joy, and God over unforgiveness look like in your life?

Day 38

Unforgiveness causes damage to you and to our time together. How do you feel when you are in a state of unforgiveness? It is not peaceful, it is not joyous, and it is void of Me. This is not how I want your life to be. I want your life to be full of joy, gladness, love, and happiness. This is impossible while you are holding on to unforgiveness. Look at all the time you spend on your resentments—so much time, so much sadness, so much unhappiness. It saddens Me greatly that you can struggle with this for so long. Move forward. I want you to forgive and get back our space. Fill your emptiness with Me. Fill it with love, peace, joy, and happiness. Be free of this burden. Unforgiveness makes your shoulders tired. Let Me carry this burden for you. My shoulders are broad. My shoulders are strong. Feel the lightness when you give this to Me. Let's fill that space with joy. It will be glorious, so walk with Me. Let's walk in peace, joy, and harmony together down the road to forgiveness.

> *Take my yoke upon you and learn from me, for I am gentle and humble in heart, and you will find rest for your souls.* (Matthew 11:29 NIV)

Are you ready to hand over your burden of unforgiveness to God?

Day 39

Forgiving those you love is easy; forgiving those you don't like is much more difficult. You will struggle forgiving some people. Pray every day to forgive all who trespass against you. The sooner you forgive someone, the less time you will spend in unforgiveness. When unforgiveness festers within, it takes much longer to forgive. Forgive daily all those who trespass against you. Doesn't it feel marvelous?

> *And forgive us our sins, just as we also have forgiven those who sin against us.*
> (Matthew 6:12)

Can you commit to praying the Lord's Prayer every day—sincerely meaning it when you offer complete forgiveness to everyone as God forgives you?

CHAPTER 3

Faith

With Me, all things are fully possible. You just have to have faith. With faith, anything can happen. Turn it over to Me.

Without faith, we are not able to surrender our lives to God. Do we really, truly believe there is a God? We don't see Him, but we see evidence of Him every day. Sometimes that evidence is as small as the dragonfly that buzzes up and looks us in the eyes. Sometimes the evidence is as large as a prayer that is miraculously answered. When we have faith, we know that God is with us every second of every day. We know that we can trust Him with our lives. I bought a sign years ago that says, "Faith is not knowing that God can; it is knowing that He will." *That* is faith. When you start having faith, the world changes before your eyes. You see things that you have never seen before. You see God's miracles every day. It is truly magnificent!

Day 40

Having 100 percent faith is truly difficult. It is very difficult to fully trust in anyone or anything—even in Me. However, those who are able to do this live joy-filled lives. People learn to turn more and more over to Me as they trust in Me and as they see the results of their faith. You have been taught by society that in order to trust, you must prove that you are trustworthy. I will prove this to you daily when you put your trust in Me! However, you must make the choice to trust and have faith in Me every day, every minute, and every second.

> *You always show me the path of life.*
> *You will fill me with joy when I am with you.*
> *You will make me happy forever at your right hand.*
> (Psalm 16:11)

Are you willing to make the choice to trust God every day, every minute, and every second? How can you begin to do this?

Day 41

You are not testing Me when you ask for help. Testing is like an ultimatum: *God, give me this, or make this happen, or I will not believe.* That is different from asking, *God, I know You can make this happen. I have no doubt.* With that type of faith and strong prayer, I know I will grant your prayer. When you pray with total faith and trust in Me, your prayers will be answered. Sometimes your prayers might not be answered in the exact way you wanted, but they will be answered.

> *So I tell you, when you pray for something, believe that you have already received it. Then it will be yours.* (Mark 11:24)

Do you only pray when you need something? Do you pray daily?

Day 42

Your faith will continue to grow. You can see My works every day and attribute them to Me. Choosing to see and recognizing My works every day is a huge step in faith. Asking Me about them is an even larger step of faith. Continue to see My works and ask Me about them.

> *The LORD has done great things for us.*
> *And we are filled with joy.* (Psalm 126:3)

Mentally list how many works you have seen from God lately.

Day 43

Faith and trust. These two words can be very difficult to live by. It is easy to say that you want to put your faith and trust in Me, but doing so can be difficult. Surrendering a situation to Me might be difficult, but always remember that I have your best interests at heart. I know the future. You do not know the future. Who better to make your decisions than Me?

> *"I know the plans I have for you," announces the* Lord. *"I want you to enjoy success. I do not plan to harm you. I will give you hope for the years to come."* (Jeremiah 29:11)

Did you ever consider that since God knows the future, maybe His way is better than yours?

Day 44

When doubt comes into play, bring yourself back to the present and ask Me to help you to have faith and trust. Say this prayer: *God, please bring me back to the present and help me to have faith and trust in You. You will do what is best for me because of Your great love for me. You know the future and the best path for me.* This simple prayer will help you to have faith and trust in Me. Also, the more you surrender and the more faith and trust in Me you have, the more you will be rewarded. The more times you surrender and it works out, the more confident you will be in Me, and the easier it will become.

> *But when you ask, you must believe. You must not doubt. That's because a person who doubts is like a wave of the sea. The wind blows and tosses them around.* (James 1:6)

How can you practice surrendering and trusting God today?

Day 45

Lead your life by My guidance. Many people seem to fight this. They want to be in control. Relinquishing control of one's life is extremely difficult, but when you figure out who is in control—Me—it is easier. Many people want to do My will but do not know how or do not know what My will is. Surrender it all to Me. View your life as a puzzle, and envision the pieces coming together. Relinquish the next piece of the puzzle to Me. Let Me pick the next piece to add to the puzzle. This might be difficult for you to do, but through faith and trust in Me, it can become easier. Do not focus on a small piece of the puzzle, but focus on the large picture that the pieces of the puzzle create—the final outcome. Trust in Me. Have faith in Me.

> *"My thoughts are not like your thoughts. And your ways are not like my ways," announces the* Lord.
> (Isaiah 55:8)

Have you ever thought of your life as being pieces of a puzzle? Does this make it easier to have faith that God sees the entire picture even though you don't?

Day 46

Trust in Me and surrender your life to Me. If you continue to do this, your life will be glorious. Be present and know that I am with you, that we are on this journey together. You are My sheep, and I am your shepherd. Let Me lead you.

> *He takes care of his flock like a shepherd.*
> *He gathers the lambs in his arms.*
> *He carries them close to his heart.*
> *He gently leads those that have little ones.*
> (Isaiah 40:11)

Can you humble yourself enough to let God shepherd you and lead your life?

Day 47

Faith is putting your entire life into My hands—surrendering everything to Me. When you are able to do that, you have true faith. At first, it is difficult to surrender even the small things in your life, but by doing the small things first, you are able to develop faith and trust in Me. Then begin to surrender larger things. When these work out for the best, your faith and trust grow stronger. Surrender the big things next, and watch them work out. Your faith and trust will grow even stronger. Then completely surrender—that is true faith and trust. Give Me your entire life—your total faith and trust. Your rewards will be glorious and beyond anything you could ever imagine.

> *Lord, those who know you will trust in you.*
> *You have never deserted those who look to you.* (Psalm 9:10)

What is something small you can surrender to God today? Are you ready to surrender something larger?

Day 48

The funny thing is that you have never had control of your life. I have control. However, you are able to make choices in your life. You have free will. Those choices sometimes lead to heartache, but making the choices I set out for you is faith. You can say that you surrender your life, but part of the surrendering is letting Me make the choices for you. This can be hard because you have blinders on and do not know what the outcome will be, but trusting and having faith in Me to make these choices and lead you blindly—that is faith.

> *We live by believing, not by seeing.*
> (2 Corinthians 5:7)

What is an example of a situation where you wish you had allowed God to make the choice for you?

Day 49

You are doing well with your faith. Let's take it one step further. Completely turning yourself over to Me is the most liberating action you can take. This is very difficult. Think how difficult it has been to surrender what you have already surrendered. However, surrendering everything to Me is complete faith. Believing that I am in control of everything is complete faith. Asking Me which way to turn at all times is complete faith.

I am the LORD your God.
I take hold of your right hand.
I say to you, "Do not be afraid.
I will help you." (Isaiah 41:13)

How would your life be different if you lived as if you truly believed that God is fully in control?

Day 50

Include Me in all your decisions. This will also keep you in My presence throughout the day. Know that I am with you all day and all night. Feel My presence next to you at all times—sitting next to you right now, next to you in the store, at the gym, walking, running. Start to become aware of My presence all the time. Start each day with this thought, and soon it will become very natural to know that I am there with you always. Don't just be in My presence but feel My presence. This will help you to keep that direct line of communication open to Me all day long. I am there to love you, to help you, to guide you, and to bless you. Start to work on this. It will take time, but you can do it.

> *Be still, and know that I am God.*
> (Psalm 46:10 NIV)

Spend today becoming still and being aware that you are in God's presence. Build upon this every day.

Day 51

Jesus and the disciples performed many miracles, but still people who saw them did not believe. It saddened Me. Blessed are those who do not see yet believe. This still has not changed today. There are many people who do not see or have not seen and still believe, and unfortunately, there are people who still do not believe.

> *Then Jesus told him, "Because you have seen me, you have believed. Blessed are those who have not seen me but still have believed."* (John 20:29)

Reflect deeply on this. Are you someone who has not seen and still believes, or are you someone who still does not believe?

Day 52

There are many reasons why people turn from Me. Much of it has to do with the idolatry of today's world. It pulls them from Me. It is so much easier to surrender to the many things of this world, such as drinking, drugs, adultery, and money, than to surrender to Me. Many people turn away and blame Me for their choices and the outcomes. I will always make sure that My children have all they need—no more, no less; this life is only temporary. The goal of this life is to get to the next life. Many people lose sight of this. That is very easy to do with all the things of this world.

> *Therefore I tell you, do not worry about your life, what you will eat or drink; or about your body, what you will wear. Is not life more than food, and the body more than clothes?*
> (Matthew 6:25 NIV)

What is one thing that you worry about that you can hand over to God right now?

Day 53

Be faithful. Be faithful in every situation that you have. When in doubt, turn to Me and be faithful. When troubled, turn to Me and be faithful. When sad, turn to Me and be faithful. When happy, turn to Me and be faithful. When life is glorious, turn to Me and be faithful. Faithfulness needs to be in your life all the time—during both the good times and the bad times. Love Me. Trust Me. I will always be here for you. Speak to Me throughout the day. Continue to show Me your faithfulness. I am so happy that you are willing to work on this and that you are willing to become closer to Me. Be My disciple.

> *Rejoice always, pray continually, give thanks in all circumstances; for this is God's will for you in Christ Jesus.* (1 Thessalonians 5:16–18 NIV)

Are you willing to be God's disciple? If so, what does that look like?

Day 54

With all the distractions of this world, having faith all the time is difficult. Many things can lead you astray—finances, heartache, work, everyday life, illness—many, many things. But when you surrender your life to Me daily, hourly, every minute, and every second, you are able to get rid of this lack of faith. Surrender yourself to Me. Let everything go. Then, as things work out, you develop deeper faithfulness by the second, minute, hour, day, and year throughout your entire life. It is really very simple, but it can seem very difficult. Surrender everything to Me, and when it all works out, faithfulness is instilled. Faithfulness is surrendering to Me, knowing that I am in control. It is really very beautiful and very calming when you do this.

> *Set your minds on things above, not on earthly things.* (Colossians 3:2 NIV)

What are some earthly distractions that keep you from fully focusing on and surrendering to God?

Day 55

It is society that pulls you away from Me. You have to work on surrendering to Me every minute, hour, day, and year. Have faith in Me. When you surrender all to Me, your life will be glorious. Faithfulness equals surrender.

> *Don't live the way this world lives. Let your way of thinking be completely changed. Then you will be able to test what God wants for you. And you will agree that what he wants is right. His plan is good and pleasing and perfect.* (Romans 12:2)

What keeps you from surrendering to God?

Day 56

Learn to put much faith in Me. That is the key: full reliance on Me—turning your life over to Me. With this faith, you will receive much peacefulness. I know this is very difficult for you to do. I understand that. But the rewards are so great. Your faith will grow every day as you surrender to Me. Let Me lead. Continue to trust Me and put your faith in Me.

> *The LORD replied, "I will go with you. And I will give you rest."* (Exodus 33:14)

Where do you most need rest and peacefulness in your life right now?

Day 57

There are many times in life when you could have become a victim. You could have become bitter. You could have blamed Me. Instead, you turned to Me and allowed Me to help you and heal you, and you became closer to Me. You make many choices every day, and I am very delighted when you choose Me—not only during times of strife, but also during times of gladness. When you pray every morning, see My beauty, and call to Me throughout the day, it delights Me because you are choosing Me. It is truly beautiful.

> *He doesn't take pleasure in the strength of horses.*
> *He doesn't take delight in the strong legs of warriors.*
> *The LORD takes delight in those who have respect for him.*
> *They put their hope in his faithful love.*
> (Psalm 147:10–11)

How are you going to choose God today?

Day 58

We have spoken so much about faith. Let's look deeper. Scripture says that faith the size of a mustard seed can move mountains. This shows that the tiniest amount of faith can do miraculous things. I know, though, that it is difficult to have faith. When you add a little more faith and are rewarded each time, faith soon becomes easier and easier. Continue to surrender your life to Me and have the faith that it will all work out. Have faith in Me, and build upon it—like a small snowball that continues to get larger and larger as it rolls along the ground. Soon it becomes indestructible! It might crumble at times, but the core stays strong. Your faith can build upon itself just as the snow does on a snowball as it is rolled. Continue to build your snowball!

> *He replied, "Because your faith is much too small. What I'm about to tell you is true. If you have faith as small as a mustard seed, it is enough. You can say to this mountain, 'Move from here to there.' And it will move. Nothing will be impossible for you."* (Matthew 17:20–21)

Do you have faith the size of a mustard seed? Why or why not?

Day 59

Those people who surrender their lives to Me have much faith in Me. This is the most amazing gift that My children give to Me. Faith in Me is so beautiful, so amazing. I know how difficult it is to have faith in today's world, yet many of My children have faith in Me.

> *Whoever believes in me, as Scripture has said,*
> *rivers of living water will flow from within them.*
> (John 7:38 NIV)

Have you considered that God sees your faith in Him as an amazing gift to Him? Have you given this gift to God?

Day 60

Faith is built. Remember that. I give examples of Me all around you and to everyone else every day. Some people don't choose to see this. They say that My works are a coincidence, or they give some other excuse. When you recognize My works in many things, your faith will be strengthened. They are a special reminder that I am with you always. I am here protecting you and guiding you.

Didn't my hand make all these things? (Acts 7:50)

What examples of God's handiwork have you already experienced today?

Day 61

Faith is the foundation of believing in Me. As it says in Scripture, *Blessed are those who have not seen Me but still have believed.* Faith and belief in Me begin at home. Many people do not know why they believe, but they believe. How do children learn? Many children are brought up in a home with no faith or belief in Me. Those kids do not believe because they have never been taught how. How sad is that? Many of them do find Me along the way, and that is one of the best miracles. I always provide access for people to learn about Me, but it is still their choice to choose Me.

> *He said to them, "Go into all the world. Preach the good news to everyone."* (Mark 16:15)

What ways can you teach others about God?

CHAPTER 4

God's Presence

Keep your eyes open,
and you will see Me often.

What is meant by "presence"? Presence is the actual presence of God with you at this very moment. God is with you always, every minute of every day. How do you recognize this? First, by faith—by truly believing that God is with you. Second, by noticing all of the beauty around you, such as the hawk flying overhead, an animal looking you in the eyes, the hummingbird that seems to stop right in front of you, the beautiful sunset—so many different ways. Third, you feel God's presence through your senses. Many people feel His presence, hear Him, smell Him—and some even see Him. All of this is done through faith. God created us to know His presence. It is society that has taught us otherwise. Learn to recognize God's presence, and your life will change forever. God wants us to know that He is truly with us all the time.

Day 62

I am the One who is always there for you. I am the One who loves you the most. I am the One who will always have your best interest at heart. Always. Have faith and believe that.

> *How can I get away from your Spirit?*
> *Where can I go to escape from you?*
> (Psalm 139:7)

People sense God's presence in different ways. How or where do you best experience the Spirit of God?

Day 63

I am always here. Sometimes you realize it and sometimes you don't, but the key is recognizing it. I am always watching over you. Many times you are not aware of My presence, but you will learn to believe it through faith. Knowing that I am with you will give you peace and comfort during difficult times.

> *You make known to me the*
> *path of life;*
> *you will fill me with joy in*
> *your presence,*
> *with eternal pleasures at*
> *your right hand.* (Psalm 16:11 NIV)

How does knowing that God is always with you bring you comfort? When do you need His presence the most?

Day 64

Be still and listen. Pay attention, and you will see that I am everywhere. You will see My beauty in all things and in all beings. Just pay attention in all that you do.

> *He says, "Be still, and know that I am God.*
> *I will be honored among the nations.*
> *I will be honored in the earth."* (Psalm 46:10)

What is one way you can regularly be still before God in order to sense His presence?

Day 65

You need to keep your mind clear of the clutter. When it is full of so many things, you will not be able to sense My presence. When you feel this way, take a step back and clear your mind. Listen to your heart. Be in the present and stop worrying about the things that are out of your control. This will help you open up your heart to Me. You can do this anywhere. Spread your tasks out, slow down, and be present.

> *But Martha was distracted by all the preparations that had to be made. She came to him and asked, "Lord, don't you care that my sister has left me to do the work by myself? Tell her to help me!"*
>
> *"Martha, Martha," the Lord answered, "you are worried and upset about many things, but few things are needed. . . . Mary has chosen what is better."* (Luke 10:40–42 NIV)

Is your mind so full of clutter, worries, and things to do that you are missing God's presence?

Day 66

I am always right beside you. To feel that, you need to continue to give Me space in your life and heart. When you are distant—pray. Call out My name. I will always answer you. I am right here. Sometimes just talking to Me will bring us closer. See Me and hear Me throughout the day. Notice My beauty. All of this will bring you closer to Me.

> *Come near to God, and he will come near to you.*
> (James 4:8)

On a scale from 0–10, with 10 being the closest you've ever felt God, how near to God do you feel today? How can you draw closer to Him?

Day 67

Being in My presence can be difficult. Things happen throughout the day to impede this. However, you can be brought back to My presence by simply taking a moment to ask, *God, are You here?* Throughout the day, practice asking if I am here. I will reassure you that I am. Take the time to look at the sky, the birds, the mountains, and nature. These show My presence. When you do this, you will find that peacefulness surrounds you. Know that I am always with you. When you do not feel peacefulness, you are not in the present. Bring yourself back to the present and feel My presence. Peacefulness will wash over you. Say a quick prayer: *Lord, please help me to be in the present and feel Your presence. Please bring me peace.* Just this short prayer will make you more aware of My presence.

> *But ask the animals what God does. They will teach you. Or ask the birds in the sky. They will tell you. Or speak to the earth. It will teach you. Or let the fish in the ocean educate you. Are there any of these creatures that don't know what the powerful hand of the* L*ORD* *has done? He holds the life of every creature in his hand. He controls the breath of every human being.* (Job 12:7–10)

Which of God's creations in nature bring you the most peace and bring you back to His presence?

Day 68

Be present in My presence. It is very important to be with Me all day and throughout the day. Throughout your day, call to Me. This will bring you back to the present with Me, especially when things get busy. I will bring you peace and calmness when this happens.

Never stop praying. (1 Thessalonians 5:17)

How can you remind yourself to call out to God during each day?

Day 69

Society can make your life very difficult. Society has made it difficult to be in the present in My presence. Society has taught you to worry about the past and the future. Society has taught you that you can't be in My presence and hear Me. It is difficult to break away from society and your worries to just be with Me. Set aside a specific time and place every day to just be with Me, to be in My presence. Soon you will progress to being with Me more and more throughout the day. It is a series of baby steps.

> *Don't worry about anything. No matter what happens, tell God about everything. Ask and pray, and give thanks to him.* (Philippians 4:6)

Are you willing to set aside a specific time every day to be with God and to be in His presence? If you have already done this, what are the results?

Day 70

I am with you every day, all day long. You are often unaware of My presence. You can become more aware of My presence when you are at peace and are in the present. All three of these are interchangeable. When you are at peace, you are in the present and you feel My presence. When you are present, you are at peace and in My presence. When you are in My presence, you are in the present and at peace. All three of the *P*s work together like legs on a stool. If you remove one, you do not have a stool, and you will fall down. It can be difficult because there are many outside influences that prevent peacefulness and being in the present, but I am always present. During the day, take the time to be present and see My presence.

> *So don't worry about tomorrow. Tomorrow will worry about itself. Each day has enough trouble of its own.* (Matthew 6:34)

Of the three *P*s—experiencing God's presence, being in the present, and having peace—which is the most difficult for you?

How can you change this?

Day 71

What about heaven on Earth? Heaven on Earth is being in My presence, being with Me. How exciting is it to be with Me now? How exciting is it to have that peace and joy now? You can have that every time you are in My presence. You can always have that feeling that you could just sit forever and be with Me. That is a slice of heaven. Those are the times when you are so much in My presence, so much with Me, that it is like heaven on Earth. As you become more in tune to Me, more in My presence, you will feel more at peace. Devote more time to Me. I am begging all of My children to spend more time with Me, to have that slice of heaven on Earth. I want this for all of My children. Yes, this is possible. Do not let your mind get in the way; totally let go. Get rid of all your thoughts and just be. Really just be. Fill your heart with Me. Release all to Me. Everything. Feel My presence. Really feel it.

> *When you pray, go into your room. Close the door and pray to your Father, who can't be seen. Your Father will reward you, because he sees what you do secretly.* (Matthew 6:6)

Will you commit more time each day to sit in God's presence?

Day 72

Be present so that you can see evidence of Me daily. You are not present when you are focusing on society and society's expectations. You are not present when you are concerned about yesterday or are worried about the future. When you are not present, you miss My presence. Be present and see My beauty. See the chirping birds, the flying hawks, the dragonflies, and even the flies. They are all evidence of Me. These are not happenstance, but these are Me. Be present and be aware. Always look for Me in your life. It makes every day truly amazing.

> *Ever since the world was created it has been possible to see the qualities of God that are not seen. I'm talking about his eternal power and about the fact that he is God. Those things can be seen in what he has made.* (Romans 1:20)

Have you noticed when you are present that you see even more evidence of God in your life?

Day 73

Have you really experienced My presence? I have given you five senses: sight, hearing, smell, touch, and taste. You can use the first four for Me. You know you can "feel" My presence, but you can also actually feel My arms around you. You can feel My touch. You can actually feel My presence and My touch. Don't be afraid of this. It is truly an amazing gift to be able to feel My presence. So in the mornings and throughout the day, actually feel My presence with you. Feel My touch and My loving arms. Do not allow your mind to tell you this cannot happen.

> *When you look for me with all your heart, you will find me.* (Jeremiah 29:13)

Did you realize that you can see, hear, smell, and feel God? Has this ever happened to you?

Day 74

Be present. Call to Me when you need help. Call to Me to say hello. Call to Me to know I am there. Call to Me. Work on being present with Me at all times. I know this is difficult, especially during busy times, but there are those quieter times when you can call to Me. Know that I am with you always. Become more aware of My presence. Become more dialed into Me.

> *You, Lord, are forgiving and good,*
> *abounding in love to all who call to you.*
> (Psalm 86:5 NIV)

How often during the day do you call to God?

Day 75

Pick yourself up. You are okay. I am with you. I am sitting beside you. Feel My presence. Feel My arms around you. I love you and am with you always.

> *You can be sure that I am always with you, to the very end.* (Matthew 28:20)

How does it make you feel to know that God is with you right now? Try to feel His presence.

Day 76

Remember that you are never alone. I am with you always. I will be there to walk this life with you, to guide you, to love you, and to give you joy. Never feel alone. Feel My presence.

> *I will ask the Father. And he will give you another friend to help you and to be with you forever. That friend is the Spirit of truth. The world can't accept him. That's because the world does not see him or know him. But you know him. He lives with you, and he will be in you.*
> (John 14:16–17)

Have you ever felt alone? Can you begin to believe that God's presence is always with you?

Day 77

Let's discuss how to get back to My presence. There are times in this journey when you begin to feel distant from Me; your faith wavers a little bit. Many things can cause this, such as stress, disappointment, and busyness. What should you do? Stop and take time for Me. When you are feeling out of sync, you are rushing your time with Me. Get up a few minutes earlier and make more time—just a little more time. This will help to bring you back to Me. During the day, you can set your alarm as a reminder to take a few minutes to just talk to Me or to admire the beauty around you. A clear indication that you are drifting away is that you will notice that your mind has started to work overtime. It could happen to you in the morning or at night. You won't be able to shut it off. It is a warning signal. When this happens, bring yourself back to Me. I will be there waiting.

> *So the Lord must wait for you to come to him so*
> *he can show you his love and compassion.*
> (Isaiah 30:18 NLT)

Is your mind working overtime? Do you feel as if you have drifted further from God? What will you do to remedy this?

CHAPTER 5

Being Present

Be loving. Be kind. Just be. Enjoy life.
Enjoy your blessings. Be kind. Just be.

Be present. What exactly does that mean? You find God in the present, not in the past or in the future. We tend to spend a lot of time replaying events of the past, but God is not in the past. We tend to worry much about the future, but God is not in the future. When we create stories about the future, they never happen the way we create them—and God never seems to be in these stories. So where is God? He is in the present—right now. God begs us to be in the present in His presence. Once you are able to be present with Him, you will be able to have a close, personal relationship with Him.

Day 78

Being present—this is one of the keys to having a personal relationship with Me. This is the key to My castle. Think of your heart as having many doors. You open one door and there is another door. You need to find the key to each door. The first door is to clear the mind. Find that key and open that door. The next door is being present. Do not worry about the past or be concerned with the future. Be present; then be still and empty and listen for My voice. Open the next door and hear My voice. Be in My presence. When you open the door to My presence, you are opening the last door to your heart, where I reside. Depending on how covered your heart is, you may have many doors to open. Some of these doors may include pain, greed, hate, judgmentalism, or lust. They all must be opened to find the heart, to find Me. There are many keys scattered around on the floor; let Me help you find the correct key. Do not be dismayed if you open a door and there is another door. The prize inside is worth finding. Together we can find the correct key. I will lead your hand to the next key. Together we will unlock the doors, and we will find the final golden key to open that last door to your heart and to My presence.

> *Here I am! I stand at the door and knock.*
> *If anyone hears my voice and opens the door,*
> *I will come in and eat with that person,*
> *and they with me.* (Revelation 3:20 NIV)

How many doors do you have covering your heart? What are they? Are you willing to allow help from God to find the keys to open the doors?

Day 79

Being. Just be. People get so tied up in what is going on—past, present, and future—that they forget to be. Be in the present. Be in life. Look around and see the beauty that I created. Look at the sky. See the trees. Hear the birds. Just be. Take a few moments every day and just be. Don't get tied up in a bunch of stuff. Just be.

> *Be still before the* LORD
> *and wait patiently for him.* (Psalm 37:7 ESV)

Where do you live the most: in the past, the future, or the present? Where do you find God?

Day 80

I am here. I am waiting. I am always here with you. Enjoy life. Enjoy the beauty of the season. Just be. I want you to concentrate on this, and you will find yourself back to where you should be—back with Me, stronger than before.

> *Return to your God! You're down*
> *but you're not out.* (Hosea 14:1–3 MSG)

Is God waiting for you?

Day 81

Live in the present. That is an easy thing to say, but it is difficult to do. Humans tend to worry about the future. This takes you out of the present.

> *Look at the birds of the air. They don't plant or gather crops. They don't put away crops in storerooms. But your Father who is in heaven feeds them. Aren't you worth much more than they are? Can you add even one hour to your life by worrying?* (Matthew 6:26–27)

Does your worry take up space from God?

Day 82

Being present is very difficult. It is so easy to worry about the future. Many of these worries do not even come to pass. The only truthfulness is in the present. Don't live in the past either. It is over and done with. You can't change the past, and yet many choose to dwell there. You cannot move forward from it. It is easy to fall into the past or the future. Living in the present can be difficult, but I am in the present—so be present, and be with Me.

> *Therefore, if anyone is in Christ,*
> *the new creation has come:*
> *The old has gone,*
> *the new is here!* (2 Corinthians 5:17 NIV)

If the only truthfulness is in the present, and that is where God is, why don't you live there?

Day 83

You need to surrender your life to Me. Do not live in the future. Be in the present where I am. Not being present is why you may feel a disconnect from Me. Give Me all your worries, stresses, and tears. Why are you worrying? That is for the future. Be calm. Be still. Be in the present. Be with Me. You will feel the peacefulness of living in the present with Me. Do not be afraid, for I am always with you. I will always take care of you. I will never leave you.

> *Be strong and courageous. Do not be afraid or terrified because of them, for the LORD your God goes with you; he will never leave you nor forsake you.* (Deuteronomy 31:6 NIV)

What is one worry that you have? Do you understand that worry keeps you from being in the present with God?

Day 84

Just be present. I love just being with you. Those who do not hear My voice often feel discouraged, but I am not discouraged. I love just being with you. I know that you have set aside this time for Me, and it delights Me. I am happy, so just enjoy our time together. It is about Me and you spending time together. When you are with your daughter/son/spouse/friends, do you need to always have conversation, or is it nice sometimes to just sit with each other? That is how I feel as well. We don't always need to be talking. Just being together is enough.

> *She had a sister called Mary, who sat at the Lord's feet listening to what he said.* (Luke 10:39 NIV)

How does it make you feel to know that God just loves being with you, that He enjoys just sitting with you?

Day 85

In the morning, your mind is very empty. Your mind begins to work as soon as you begin to think about your day, watch the news, read the headlines, check social media, or talk to your spouse. It begins to take up space from Me. That is why you should spend time with Me first thing in the morning before your brain takes off and you get into your day.

> *Let the morning bring me word*
> *of your unfailing love,*
> *for I have put my trust in you.*
> *Show me the way I should go,*
> *for to you I entrust my life.* (Psalm 143:8 NIV)

What changes do you need to make so that your day starts with God on a regular basis?

Day 86

Continue to see your surroundings. Do not just see My beauty, but see the beauty in others too. See the good in everyone and everything. Take a moment to smell the flowers. When you take these moments, you are closer to Me.

> *Be completely gentle. Be patient.*
> *Put up with one another in love.* (Ephesians 4:2)

How can seeing the good in others bring you closer to God?

Day 87

All that I ask is that you do your best. See the best in people. See what people are all about. See their beauty. See their love. With some people, you really have to dig beneath the layers to see their true beauty. Time and situations have covered them up, so take the time to find their beauty. Remember that they are all My children and that I am within them.

> *Accept the person whose faith is weak. Don't argue with them where you have differences of opinion.* (Romans 14:1)

Is there someone in your life with whom you need to dig deeper to find their beauty?

Day 88

Do you hear the birds? So many people go through life and don't hear the birds. They do not see the beauty in nature and do not appreciate nature. I am glad you see it. So much happens in nature—so much beauty.

> *The heavens tell about the glory of God.*
> *The skies show that his hands created them.*
> (Psalm 19:1)

What does nature tell us about the character of God?

Day 89

People need to open their eyes and see Me all around them. People get so busy with their lives that they forget to see the essence of life. They don't enjoy life. They don't see My beauty. They don't hear the birds. They don't see the flowers. It is very sad because they are missing out on the simplest ways to experience Me.

> *Let the heavens rejoice, let the earth be glad;*
> *let the sea resound, and all that is in it.*
> *Let the fields be jubilant, and everything in them;*
> *let all the trees of the forest sing for joy.*
> (Psalm 96:11–12 NIV)

Take time to listen to the joy of the birds. Do you see God in them? Do you see God's hand in all beauty?

Day 90

Be open. Let everything go. If you are not open, you will not be able to hear Me. Just be completely empty. I know that is difficult, but be open to hear what I have to say.

> *Whoever is of God hears the words of God.*
> (John 8:47 ESV)

Are you open to listening to and hearing God?

Day 91

Just be. Learn to be present. How? Notice the beauty around you—My beauty. Notice the sky, the sunrise, the sunset, the clouds, the moon, the stars, the colors—all the beautiful paintings you see every day, all day long. When you look outside, see all the colors. Begin to notice the trees, the green blades of grass, and the singing birds. See My beauty. This will help you to be. Just be.

> *Lift up your eyes on high and see: who created these? He who brings out their host by number, calling them all by name, by the greatness of his might and because he is strong in power, not one is missing.* (Isaiah 40:26 ESV)

Have you tried to spend time in nature as a way to be more present with God?

CHAPTER 6

Peace and Peacefulness

Trusting in Me brings amazing peace!

Peace and peacefulness are something that everyone desires—but how do you get there? It is a simple answer: by being present with God. However, that can be difficult because life gets in the way every day—especially if you are spending your time living in the past or worrying about the future. God just asks us for space. When we give Him this space, wondrous things happen. You begin to notice God in everything from nature to the glimmer in people's eyes. Then, as incredible things happen, you find peace. Finding and giving God space are things that we need to practice every day. God wants you to surrender your life to Him, to let Him do the worrying and let Him help you deal with the past and the future. Let Him take your anxieties away through surrender. Then you are with Him, and you will receive peace.

Day 92

Peacefulness. That is something everyone desires. When you are at peace, you are in the present. It is when you are in the past or are worried about the future that you lose peace. People who constantly worry are not at peace because they are not in the present. My desire for My children is for them to be in the present, to have faith and trust in Me, and to have peace. Sometimes worries creep in; when they do, call to Me so I can help you stop worrying. I will always reassure you that I am here, that I will take care of you and guide your life. Just call My name, and I will be there. I am here. This alone can bring your peace.

> *LORD, you will give perfect peace to those who commit themselves to be faithful to you. That's because they trust in you.* (Isaiah 26:3)

When you were worrying, did you try to call to God for help? What happened?

Day 93

No matter what is happening in your life, you strive for peacefulness. You may not know this, but you want peacefulness. Peacefulness comes after forgiveness, letting go of the past, and letting go of the future. Many people let unforgiveness disrupt their peacefulness. Think of how much not forgiving someone and living in the past have cost you in peacefulness. The other person does not know, nor does that person usually care that you are dwelling in the past in unforgiveness. They are going on about their lives. However, this unforgiveness has a hold on you and your heart and your peacefulness. Not only does unforgiveness destroy your peacefulness, but it adds a layer over your heart. It takes you further from Me.

> *I leave my peace with you. I give my peace to you. I do not give it to you as the world does. Do not let your hearts be troubled. And do not be afraid.* (John 14:27)

Are you being kept from your peace by failing to forgive someone?

Day 94

Be peaceful. Others will see your peacefulness. They will see your light. They do not know what it is, but they want it. Keep calm. Be present. Be peaceful and feel My presence. Keep calm and know that you are in My presence.

> *Blessed are the peacemakers, for they will be called children of God.* (Matthew 5:9 NIV)

Do you see peacefulness in others? Do others see peacefulness in you?

Day 95

Worrying about time and putting too much on your plate create havoc. This will take away your peace. When you fill up all of your time, you lose all of your space for Me. Then you will lose your peacefulness. Keep time and space open for Me, and keep that peacefulness. Stay in the present, in My presence, and you will have peace. You get so worried about time. Let some of that "stuff" go. Spend time with Me and feel peace. Surrender it to Me. I will take care of you and lead you down the right path. Trust in Me. As soon as you turn it all over to Me, your peacefulness will return.

> *Now return to the* L*ORD* *your God, for He is gracious and compassionate, slow to anger, abounding in lovingkindness.*
> (Joel 2:13 NASB1995)

Do you fill up all of your time, leaving no time for God? How can you return to Him?

Day 96

Just being in My presence will bring you peace. Relax and enjoy the moment. Be peaceful; it is truly a gift.

> *Now the Lord is the Holy Spirit. And where the Spirit of the Lord is, freedom is also there.*
> (2 Corinthians 3:17)

Do you feel the freedom and peace of being in God's presence?

Day 97

You experience peacefulness more and more as your journey with Me deepens. I want you to know, though, that society will get in the way and your peacefulness will descend into chaos. It is the ebb and flow of life. We will work together to bring back peacefulness. Like the waves of the ocean breaking on the beach—when they break, there is chaos. There is the white water, the sand, and the noise, but after the waves break, peacefulness comes. Then another wave comes, and more chaos. There is low tide when the waves are more gentle, and there is high tide when the waves are more violent, but peacefulness always comes again. Just as in life, the amount and strength of the chaos varies, but there is always peace after the chaos. Chaos can be beautiful when you and I work together to bring about peacefulness again. The chaos of life is an opportunity to bring beauty to our relationship. Through chaos comes beauty.

> *Commit your life to the Lord.*
> *Here is what he will do if you trust in him.*
> *He will make the reward for your godly life shine like the dawn.*
> *He will make the proof of your honest life shine like the sun at noon.* (Psalm 37:5-6)

When you reflect on the past waves in your life, do you see the beauty that came after the chaos?

Day 98

Peacefulness. You are surrounded by it in the morning. Enjoy it. This is why being with Me in the morning is so important. Feel the peacefulness around you before the world awakens. Hear the singing of the birds before the world awakens. Observe the quietness of the world before the world awakens. It is simply peacefulness. As the world awakens, so does the chaos of the day. You can no longer hear the birds singing. There are planes flying overhead, cars passing by, lawnmowers, kids—the noise of the world begins to happen. Demands of children, people in your families, work, phones—everything covers up the peacefulness. So enjoy the peacefulness of the morning with Me before the world awakens.

> *Lord, in the morning you hear my voice.*
> *In the morning I pray to you.*
> *I wait for you in hope.* (Psalm 5:3)

Do you feel the peacefulness of the morning before the day begins? Do you hear peace in silence?

Day 99

Take time to be with Me. Instead of "me" time, call it "us" time. Remember this feeling of peace, and hold on to it like precious gold or silver. Hold on tightly or the thief will steal it when you are not looking. Make your house strong and fortified. Start with the foundation, and build it on solid ground. Continue to build and fortify it from the ground up. Finish your roof. Don't neglect the maintenance of our house. It will need paint and eventually a new roof. Weeds will need to be pulled. Shrubs will need to be replaced so they don't overgrow and take over. Your house may be strong but it still needs upkeep. And yes, that upkeep is Me!

> *A thief comes only to steal and kill and destroy. I have come so they may have life. I want them to have it in the fullest possible way.* (John 10:10)

Do you allow the "thief" to come and steal your "us" time?

Day 100

You are searching quite hard for peace, and you desire peace. You do have peace; it's here and now in the present every day! When do you not have peace? When you are living in the future. When you are living in the present with Me, you can always have peace. Will you have difficulties? Of course! That is part of life, but you can have peace during these difficulties if you remember that I am here right now with you. We will go through all your difficulties together, and during those difficulties, you will have peace!

> *God is our place of safety. He gives us strength.*
> *He is always there to help us in times of*
> *trouble.* (Psalm 46:1)

Do you understand that life is full of difficulties? Will you begin to let God help you and walk with you through these difficulties?

Day 101

Faith and peacefulness. When you are always worried about the future or dwelling in the past, you are not at peace. Surrender your past to Me, and surrender your worries about the future to Me. This will put you in the present. This will give you peacefulness. Peacefulness is being in the present in My presence. I do not reside in the future or in the past, but I am in the present. Therefore, peacefulness comes to you in the present where I am. Come and be with Me in the present! Be with Me in your heart. Be with Me in your soul. I will take care of you, but you need to come and meet Me.

Think of this journey as traveling down a road. There is the part behind you—the past. Don't look back. Don't turn around. There is the part where you are going. That is the future. You do not know what is around the bend, but I do—so why not walk with Me? Let Me take care of the future. The only thing that is real is where you are standing right now on that road. Stand with Me. Be with Me. This is the point of peacefulness. Put your faith and trust in Me. Don't look back. Walk with Me. Let Me worry about what is around the bend. Surrender to Me. This will bring you peace. The present, peacefulness, and My presence are all easily obtained by standing with Me on the road.

> *Do not be anxious about anything, but in every situation, by prayer and petition, with thanksgiving, present your requests to God. And*

> *the peace of God, which transcends all understanding, will guard your hearts and your minds in Christ Jesus.* (Philippians 4:6–7 NIV)

When you stand on the road, are you looking back or looking forward—or are you standing with God in the present?

Day 102

Through faith and trust in Me, you are given peacefulness. Peacefulness is beautiful. Once you are at peace, you can enjoy My beauty. You can see My beauty with peacefulness, and it will come with calmness. You can hear Me. You can rule with your heart and not with your mind. This is beautiful, and this is My desire for all of My children.

> *But the* Lord *said to him, "Peace! Do not be afraid."* (Judges 6:23 NIV)

Which one puts you more at peace: the heart or the mind?

Day 103

Let's dive further into peace. Let's consider total surrender. When you totally surrender your life to Me, you experience total peace. Total peace is magnificent. You can experience much peace, but there is still another level. Turning your life over to Me 100 percent will give you a peace that you never thought existed.

> *Do what you have learned or received or heard from me. Follow my example. The God who gives peace will be with you.* (Philippians 4:9)

Are you experiencing total peace? What is holding you back?

Day 104

Sometimes peacefulness can be difficult. It can be difficult because you are not used to it. The mind wants to be busy, concerning itself with matters, whether big or small. But in peacefulness, the mind searches for things to think about but cannot find anything—so the result is peacefulness. Embrace this feeling because it is few and far between in this busy world. This is something many strive for, but it eludes them. Many people are just too busy to find peace.

You tend to put too much on your plate and cannot see the entrée—Me. All the foods blend together, giving a bland taste. You are unable to taste the individual foods. But with peacefulness, the plate is clear. There is an entrée (Me) and a few small sides. They are not mixed together. You can see all of the food clearly. However, when there is so much on your plate that you are unable to see the individual food items, peacefulness eludes you. Allow Me to be your entrée, and life will become more and more delicious.

> *Taste and see that the LORD is good;*
> *blessed is the one who takes refuge in him.*
> (Psalm 34:8 NIV)

What can you take off your plate so you can see your entrée?

Day 105

Sometimes peace is doing nothing—no plans, just doing nothing. There is so much peace in emptiness, but many people do not see that. They believe they always need to be doing something with their time, always filling every minute. Do you understand the opportunity in peace—in quietness, relaxation, and zero stress? Enjoy peace when you have it, for it is easy to lose. Protect your peace like it is a rare jewel. Don't let anyone steal it. Put it in a safe that has four strong iron walls, a roof, and a floor. Let Me have the combination. Covet your jewel. See the jewel shine. It has so many facets, just like Me. I am the light shining in the jewel.

> *Be alert and of sober mind. Your enemy the devil prowls around like a roaring lion looking for someone to devour.* (1 Peter 5:8 NIV)

What steps are you taking right now to guard your peace? How can you add to this?

Day 106

It is through the storms that you realize how wonderful peace truly is. Sometimes the storms are large, and other times they are small. Remember, though, that after the storm comes calmer waters.

> *You have been a refuge for the poor,*
> *a refuge for the needy in their distress,*
> *a shelter from the storm.* (Isaiah 25:4 NIV)

Have you experienced peace after a storm? When?

Day 107

Being content is a good thing. It is calmness and peace. Know, though, that another wave will come. Do not fear the next wave, for I will be there with you. Do not get complacent in your journey. When things are calm, people have a tendency to push Me away. They think they no longer need Me until the next wave comes. However, many of My children who seek help in times of need have also learned the glory of being with Me all of the time. This is how you can develop a close relationship with Me. You need to be with Me during both the good and the bad. If you are only with Me during the bad times, you are unable to develop this relationship fully. I am happy you turn to Me in times of strife, but I am even happier when you turn to Me all the time. This is truly a relationship with Me. Put Me at the center of your life always, and find peace and contentment.

> *I know what it is to be in need, and I know what it is to have plenty. I have learned the secret of being content in any and every situation, whether well fed or hungry, whether living in plenty or in want. I can do all this through him who gives me strength.* (Philippians 4:12–13 NIV)

Do you desire a close relationship with God? Are you only with God during the bad times of your life, or are you with Him during both the good and the bad times?

Day 108

True peace is total union with Me. You know peace when you and I are together. You feel peace. Realize that most people do not even have peace a small percentage of the time. This is sad to Me. Peace is realized through Me by spending time with Me and taking time during the day to be with Me. Treasure this peace always. Embrace this peace, for it helps you combat the chaos of life. Think of life as a bucket filled with the water of peace—the giving, loving water of Me. When chaos happens, a hole is punched in the bucket and the water seeps out. Some holes are bigger than others, so you need to continually fill the bucket with peace and with Me. Allow Me to plug the holes and slow the leak. What happens when the bucket runs dry? There is no water to feed the soul, resulting in much stress and anxiety. Soon the bucket becomes dry, and it cracks and breaks in pieces. Sometimes small pieces break off; eventually the entire bucket cracks. Be with Me so that we can keep your bucket full and you will be at peace.

> *Nevertheless, I will bring health and healing to it; I will heal my people and will let them enjoy abundant peace and security.*
> (Jeremiah 33:6 NIV)

Are you allowing God to keep your bucket of life full?

Day 109

When someone finally accepts Me, understands Me, and figures out that I am truly real, I truly become a part of their life. There comes an internal peace, a warming of the heart, a burden lifted, and a joy that cannot be explained. Many times it is so emotional that tears stream down their faces—tears of relief, tears of joy. The tears are a cleansing, a baptism of sorts. The emotion involved shows the joy in the heart. There is absolutely nothing that compares to this joy, this deep emotion! There is such joy and peace. It is such a gift—a gift that everyone has, yet which some people choose not to unwrap. It just sits there. It is tempting at times to open it, but it is just not unwrapped. The gift is always there, though, just waiting to be opened. It is the most joyous gift of all.

> *Tears of joy will stream down their faces,*
> *and I will lead them home with great care.*
> *They will walk beside quiet streams*
> *and on smooth paths where they will not*
> *stumble.* (Jeremiah 31:9 NLT)

Do you desire this internal joy? Have you allowed yourself to unwrap this beautiful gift, or is it still waiting to be opened?

Day 110

Peace. You understand the value of it. It is not something you should allow others to steal or take away. Have you allowed others to take away your peace? Have you allowed them to pry open your fingers that are holding on to it? Call to Me for help, and I will put My hand over yours and help you hold on to the peace. Remember that it is a choice to tightly hold on to it or to allow your fingers to be pried open. If you need help, call to Me, and I will help you hold on to it!

> *For Christ himself has brought peace to us.*
> (Ephesians 2:14 NLT)

When have you allowed others to steal God's gift of peace from you?

Day 111

Peacefulness is what I want for you. Don't lose peace; hold on to it like a precious gift of gold. I know there will be those who will try to pry it out of your hand. Don't allow them to. They will pull one finger at a time, weakening your grip. Do not allow this! Five fingers holding the gold is much stronger than four fingers, and so forth, so don't allow anyone to lessen your grip. How is this done? This is done with My strength holding your hand even tighter. Surrender to Me, let Me be in control, and let Me help keep the peace in your hand.

> *The thoughts of a person ruled by sin bring death. But the mind ruled by the Spirit brings life and peace.* (Romans 8:6)

Have you ever felt your peacefulness slipping away? Have you ever called to God and asked for help in holding on to your peace?

Day 112

Let's talk about this gift of peace. Every time a finger is pried open, there is a lesson to be learned. Not only is there a lesson for you in surrendering it to Me and pushing your finger closed again, but there is a lesson about yourself. Always dig deep to find that lesson. Speak to Me about it, and you will learn. Each lesson you learn makes it easier the next time—easier to keep those fingers closed, holding on to peace. Look back at when your peace was taken and consider the lessons learned. It often takes time before you see the lesson, but you can just ask Me, and we will walk through the lesson together. This will also bring peace.

> *They must turn away from evil and do good.*
> *They must look for peace and go after it.*
> (1 Peter 3:11)

What have you learned from having your peace stolen in the past?

Day 113

We have learned about peacefulness. Today, let's learn about the opposite—chaos. Chaos is taking over the world. Many people have overextended themselves. There is not enough time in the day to get things done. What does that lead to? It leads to chaos and impatience, both of which are not wonderful attributes. Along with this come short tempers, anger, sadness, depression, and insomnia. Many difficult things come with this busyness. There are times when you overextend yourself and you become a victim to your busyness. It is tough to take things off your plate. Learn to say no to doing things. You may feel that because you are organized, you can do more things than most people, but this is also dangerous because then you really do more, and this leads to impatience and chaos. Do you see this? When you take some things off your plate, though, life is easier. People with no time for Me exhibit anger, meanness, and impatience. They don't even have time for an hour of church. Clear out your schedule to make time for Me, to make the commitment. This will bring peace, happiness, joy, and contentment. Schedule Me first, and then everything else.

> *Does a young woman forget all about her jewelry?*
> *Does a bride forget her wedding jewels?*
> *But my people have forgotten me more days than anyone can count.* (Jeremiah 2:32)

What can you do to ensure that you never forget to schedule time with God?

Day 114

If you were always at peace, then you would not recognize peace. Unfortunately, there are those who are always in chaos and do not know peace at all. That is truly sad. Those who are in constant chaos don't even know they are in chaos. This is the law of opposites. It applies to many people. Those who are in constant anger do not know peace and calmness. Those who are in constant hate do not know love. Those who are in constant greed do not know generosity—and the list goes on. So when you see people who are continually in the negative, know that they are not even aware of it, for they do not know the positive opposite. It is so sad. Pray for them, for they know not what they do. Pray that they get a glimpse of love/My heart/Me so they can strive for it. Pray that when they see your peace, love, kindness, compassion, and love of Me that they will simply desire that and begin to change, begin to embrace the opposite, and begin to embrace Me. I will be there with open arms to love them!

> *Deceit is in the hearts of those who plot evil, but those who promote peace have joy.*
> (Proverbs 12:20 NIV)

Who can you pray for today that they may begin to seek God's peace?

CHAPTER 7

Surrender

Come and run with Me. Feel the freedom. It is truly glorious. Picture yourself running across a meadow filled with flowers, with the sun shining, the wind in your hair, total freedom, true beauty, true glory, and not a care in the world. This is heaven on Earth.

Surrender—it so easy to say but so difficult to do. Why is this? Control. We truly believe that we are in control of our lives, and we often think that we are also in control of the lives of others. When we finally accept that we are not in control, we are able to surrender to God. Then many beautiful things happen. The stress of our lives is replaced with peace. God wants us to surrender to Him and allow Him to carry our burdens. Sometimes the burdens become so heavy that we lose all peace. We worry about the past, we worry about the future, and we begin to worry about everything. God wants us to know that He has our lives under His control. However, to fully know the peace the comes with this, we must fully surrender. We must surrender control that we never even had in the first place. Why not make life so much easier and surrender to God, who knows you better than anyone? Why not surrender to the One who knows the future, loves us the most, and has our best interests in mind?

Day 115

Wonderful things happen through great faith. Putting your trust in Me and believing in Me is so easy and makes your life so much easier. It is a very beautiful experience when you surrender to Me and have the faith that things will turn out well. The more you surrender to Me, the deeper your faith will grow, and the more I will reward you.

> *Brothers and sisters, God has shown you his mercy. So I am asking you to offer up your bodies to him while you are still alive. Your bodies are a holy sacrifice that is pleasing to God. When you offer your bodies to God, you are worshiping him in the right way.* (Romans 12:1)

Have you ever surrendered to God and watched your faith grow? When?

Day 116

Go one step further than having the faithfulness to surrender. Surrender everything to Me. Consult with Me on everything throughout your day. Consult with Me about everything—not just about the big stuff. When anything comes up during the day, ask Me for direction. This is the next step to total surrender. Trust Me with your life and have faith in Me. Turn to Me. Be in My presence all day long—not just in the morning, but all day long. Get guidance from Me. Start just a little at a time and build on this. You will become dependent on My teachings and on My desire for you to have true peace in your life. You will realize that I am truly right beside you all day long. Realize the peace you have in the morning; how glorious it is to have this peace throughout the day!

> *Trust in the Lord with all your heart.*
> *Do not depend on your own understanding.*
> (Proverbs 3:5)

Do you surrender the small stuff to God? Do you surrender the big stuff to God? Which is easier? Why?

Day 117

Faith is learned. Society has taught you not to have faith, not to trust. Faith and trust in Me are learned and strengthened over time when things work out. You see the results of your faith through all of My blessings. Then you understand why you should put your faith in Me.

> *And we know that in all things God works for the good of those who love him, who have been called according to his purpose.*
> (Romans 8:28 NIV)

How has your faith in God become stronger? Do you see your many blessings?

Day 118

When you learn that you do not have control over your life, when you relinquish what control you think you have, when you finally surrender to Me—amazing and wonderful things will happen. I know how difficult it can be to relinquish control. It is very difficult, but I know you can do it!

> *Turn your worries over to the Lord.*
> *He will keep you going.*
> *He will never let godly people be shaken.*
> (Psalm 55:22)

What is the biggest control issue that keeps you from fully surrendering to God?

Day 119

Learn that you are not in control of your life. Understand that I will take care of you if you let Me. I will ease many burdens, many worries, many fears, and many stresses. Because of your free choice, many choices you make are contrary to the plan I have for you. Sometimes you take the rocky road instead of the smooth road, but eventually you get on the right path, and all along I have been here with you taking care of you.

> *In all your ways obey him.*
> *Then he will make your paths smooth*
> *and straight.* (Proverbs 3:6)

Do you find yourself on the rocky road instead of the smooth road? If so, why do you think that is?

Day 120

Surrender is the key, but surrender is a process—not just a one-time deal. You have your major surrenders and smaller surrenders, but it is an easier life when you let Me carry your burdens. Surrendering everything to Me makes your life so much more peaceful and so much less stressful.

> *The Lord will fight for you. Just be still.*
> (Exodus 14:14)

Where in your life right now do you need to *just be still* and surrender?

Day 121

Surrendering your life to Me will make your life so much easier, and it will always work out for the best. It may not be the way you anticipated it, but it will be the way that is best—it will be My way. Realizing that you are not in control of your life, that I am, takes much stress off you! Your life is much more peaceful. Do not just surrender the big events in life, but surrender the little ones as well. Remember—you are not in control; society just leads you to believe this. Once you realize this, life is much easier and is so much more peaceful!

> *"My thoughts are not like your thoughts.*
> *And your ways are not like my ways,"*
> *announces the* Lord. (Isaiah 55:8)

What is an example of a time when you had to accept God's way when you didn't believe it was best but later discovered that it was?

Day 122

I am proud of you and love you so deeply. Let Me, as the strong father, take care of all of your burdens. Just hand them off to Me. Think of Me as Hercules, and know that My strength will pull you through. Let Me not just take your burdens off your plate, but let Me take them off the table and put them into the trash. Let me give them to the dogs to devour. Let Me do this for you, for your burdens are too heavy for you to carry. You are strong, but even the strong have their limits on what they can carry. So let Me take your burdens.

> *Come to me, all you who are weary and burdened, and I will give you rest.*
> (Matthew 11:28 NIV)

What burdens can you surrender to God right now to give you rest?

Day 123

Do your best to live in Me, to trust in Me, and to surrender all to Me. I know it is difficult. I understand that. I see the pain your burdens cause you. If you could just let it all go, if you could just let Me carry your baggage, if you could just trust it all with Me—your burdens would be so much lighter. Let them go. I will protect you in all aspects of your life!

> *But let all those who go to you for safety be glad.*
> *Let them always sing for joy.*
> *Spread your cover over them and keep them safe.*
> *Then those who love you will be glad because of you.* (Psalm 5:11)

Instead of clinging to your burdens, how can you let them go, allowing God to put His cover over you?

Day 124

Continue to surrender to Me. Continue to see the fruits of surrender. Think about a fruit tree. It surrenders to the sun, rain, and weather, and every year it bears fruit. Depending on the external circumstances, some years it bears more fruit than other years. It is the same with you. Sometimes the fruits of surrender are greater depending on the external circumstances. But nonetheless, there is fruit. Sometimes a frost comes and kills much fruit, but the next year the tree produces more fruit. A fruit tree totally surrenders to Me every year—all year long. So surrender to Me all year long and enjoy the fruit.

> *The fruit of the Spirit is love, joy, peace, patience, kindness, goodness, faithfulness, gentleness, self-control.* (Galatians 5:22–23 ESV)

Are you able to be more like the fruit tree and surrender your life to God?

Day 125

Surrender can start small. It can begin with a small event in your life. When you see how that works out, you surrender a larger event. I know this is difficult because you like to think you are in control of things, but you are not; I am. Then there is total surrender—surrendering all aspects of your life to Me all day, every day. This is the greatest gift of love you can give Me. It is not just love, but it is also trust and faith. I know this is difficult, but you can do it. Call to Me for help when you are feeling overwhelmed. Surrendering all events leads to total surrender. It is like a bunch of stairs. Each step is an event, and as you step on each step, you surrender it to Me. Some steps may be shallower, some deeper, some shorter, and some taller, but surrender each step to Me and move to the next one. Soon you will see how far you have come. Continue to surrender each step. Who is at the top? Me. So give up each day to Me—one event, one step at a time.

Let your eyes look straight ahead.
Keep looking right in front of you.
Think carefully about the paths that your feet walk on.
Always choose the right ways.
Don't turn to the right or left.
Keep your feet from the path of evil.
(Proverbs 4:25–27)

What is the next step or event that you need to surrender to God?

Day 126

Continue to surrender your life to Me. Continue to climb the steps. The steps will get smaller for a while. I know they can be steep and slippery. The more you surrender, the easier the steps are to climb. So grab My hand and let Me help you climb. Let me relieve some of the pressure and the ache in your legs. It is like an incline. There are many different-sized steps—some close together and shallow, and some so far apart and steep that you need to stretch to climb up. The steep steps are much easier when you are able to reach out and grab My hand. The view at the top is glorious! Climb, My child, climb. Take the journey to the top. Let's climb together.

> *So I will lead them along paths*
> *they had not known before.*
> *I will guide them on roads they are not familiar with.*
> *I will turn the darkness into light as they travel.*
> *I will make the rough places smooth.*
> *Those are the things I will do.*
> *I will not desert my people.* (Isaiah 42:16)

What rough or steep place are you facing right now that you to need to reach out and grab God's hand?

Day 127

Picture using the elliptical machine at the gym. We climb together. When it is difficult, you close your eyes and ask Me for help. You are so tired. You are so empty of distractions that you can see Me and hear Me clearly. I am next to you, and you are able to zero in on Me. All of your senses—sight, smell, sound, taste, and touch—will become sharpened. We will become more in union, and it will be glorious! Do not fear this. It will be the most beautiful thing in the world. Think about how it feels when you hear Me. It will be beyond that. It will be joy beyond measure. Trust Me. Continue to climb.

> *The Lord gives me strength. He is like a shield*
> *that keeps me safe.*
> *My heart trusts in him, and he helps me.*
> *My heart jumps for joy.*
> *With my song I praise him.* (Psalm 28:7)

What type of relationship with God does your heart desire?

Day 128

Everyone needs a wake-up call once in a while. That is okay. Remember that each day is mine, so surrender it to Me. Let Me take care of all of your worries. I know this is difficult, but once you surrender it all to Me, it becomes easier. Let Me carry your burdens. You fight this because you think you know what is best, but in your heart, you know that I know what is best for you, for I know your inner desires—so follow Me!

> *Humble yourselves, therefore, under the mighty hand of God so that at the proper time he may exalt you, casting all your anxieties on him, because he cares for you.* (1 Peter 5:6–7 ESV)

Do you fight surrender because you believe you know what is best? How can you turn over your anxieties to God?

Day 129

Trust Me. Take a deep breath and know that I am sitting right here beside you. Be like a child sitting on her father's lap in trying times. I will hold you and give you strength. Imagine the power and glory in that! With Me, how can it go wrong? Just as children trust their fathers, so too you can trust in Me, your true Father. Feel My strength as I hold you and protect you. How simple it is to just surrender and have faith and trust in Me! I know it is difficult because you do not see the future, but always remember that I do! I will take care of those who surrender to Me!

> *A father is tender and kind to his children.*
> *In the same way, the Lord is tender and kind*
> *to those who have respect for him.*
> (Psalm 103:13)

Do you trust God as a child trusts his father?

Day 130

Life on Earth is a constant uphill climb. Sometimes the climb is rocky and steep, and other times you are on a plateau, but it is always a climb. It is a climb to Me. When you slip, you can either put your hand out so I can grab it and pull you back, or you can put both your hands down to stop your fall. With both hands down, you are in control of when and where you stop, but with both hands up, or even with one hand up, you are with Me, trusting Me to help you up.

> *Immediately Jesus reached out his hand and caught him. "You of little faith," he said, "why did you doubt?" And when they climbed into the boat, the wind died down.* (Matthew 14:31–32 NIV)

Do you trust God enough to raise your hands to Him when you fall, or do you trust yourself more to stop your fall?

Day 131

Remember that surrender is a daily thing, an hourly thing, a minute-by-minute thing. Just work on that today.

> *So do not fear, for I am with you; do not be dismayed, for I am your God. I will strengthen you and help you; I will uphold you with my righteous right hand.* (Isaiah 41:10 NIV)

Are you willing to start your surrender today?

Day 132

My wish for you is to be at peace with Me, so make the choice for peace, and rest your weary head with Me, on My shoulder. Let Me be your strength; let Me be your healing. I will take care of all of your struggles. Sometimes the road to happiness includes a bypass through sadness.

> *Therefore we do not lose heart. Though outwardly we are wasting away, yet inwardly we are being renewed day by day.* (2 Corinthians 4:16 NIV)

When in your life has the road to happiness included a bypass through sadness?

Day 133

Sometimes you feel exhausted with life. Ask, and I will pull you out of the waves and onto the shore to rest—to rest and bask in the sun, to relax and find peace. This is just on the horizon, so hang in there for a few more waves. Peace will come. I will surf with you. The waves may appear large, but with Me, the ride will be glorious. One last ride before the rest—one last ride.

> *For our light and momentary troubles are achieving for us an eternal glory that far outweighs them all.* (2 Corinthians 4:17 NIV)

What wave are you fighting right now? Will you surf with God to peace?

Day 134

Continue to surrender your life to Me in all situations. I will continue to take care of you! I love you and am proud of you. I am so proud of the person you are becoming. Continue on this wonderful highway of life. Sometimes you take an exit from the highway and discover it to be quite bumpy and uncomfortable. Then you veer back onto the smooth pavement and see how smooth and glorious it is! Remember that when you feel out of sorts, you are on a side road. It is curvy and bumpy and not well maintained. Feel the calmness now of the smooth road. That is when you know you are back on the highway with Me.

> *Have I not commanded you? Be strong and courageous. Do not be afraid; do not be discouraged, for the* Lord *your God will be with you wherever you go.* (Joshua 1:9 NIV)

Can you tell when you have veered off the road with God? How can you veer back?

Day 135

Once you experience the power of surrender, you will desire it even more, just as it is with love. If you did not know love, you would not desire it. But once you know love, you want it. This is why I tell My children to surrender a little bit to Me at a time. Then when it works out, you will want to surrender more things—the bigger things. Until you try it and see that it works, though, you don't know what you are missing. It is kind of like a delicious piece of chocolate cake. If you have never tried it, you don't know what you are missing! So try the cake/surrender, and see how wonderful it truly is!

> *I sought the Lord, and he answered me; he delivered me from all my fears.* (Psalm 34:4 NIV)

Are you afraid to surrender to God? Why? Are you willing to try?

Day 136

When you feel the heavy burden of the strife of those you love, call to Me and I will help you. I give you permission to surrender them to Me. There is no guilt in surrendering those whom you love. This doesn't mean you don't care. Release them to Me and let it go. Often, there is nothing you can do anyway except to ask for prayer and support. Don't confuse this support with carrying the burden. Those are two different things. You might feel that you are no longer caring or concerned if you surrender them to Me, but that is not it at all. In fact, surrendering is actually helping them since you are able to think more clearly. This is even greater help. The worry puts a fog around your vision. It clogs your clarity. Releasing the burdens also provides clarity of the situation. You do a better service to those you love when you can see clearly. You are driving on a sunny day instead of a foggy, drizzly day. So when you feel or see the fog, call to Me, surrender, and see clearly.

> *The righteous cry out, and the Lord hears them;*
> *he delivers them from all their troubles.*
> (Psalm 34:17 NIV)

Do you trust God to take care of those whom you love when they need Him? Then why are you carrying their burdens?

Day 137

Do you feel that you do not care enough if your loved ones in strife are not heavy on your heart? Do you believe that you are not caring if you are having fun in your life? Do you think that you are not caring if you don't think about them every day? You need to understand that you do not need to carry their burdens. Yes, love and pray for them, but don't feel guilty if you are enjoying yourself and having fun. Remember, this is not your burden to carry. When you are worried all the time, you are not trusting Me to take care of them. You are taking on the burden. It is not your burden to carry.

> *I will say to the* Lord, *"My refuge and my fortress, my God, in whom I trust."* (Psalm 91:2 ESV)

Do you understand the difference between carrying their burden and surrendering them to God? Do you trust God to carry the burdens of those you love?

CHAPTER 8

Joy and Happiness

It is through Me that people find happiness.

Joy and happiness are things that we all strive to have in our lives. However, many of us do not have these. Why not? The root of joy and happiness is being in union with God. God wants us to be joyful, to have a little slice of heaven on Earth, but we continually allow outside circumstances to steal away our joy and happiness. We allow others to add stress and anxiety to our lives. We live in the past and worry about the future. We do not surrender our lives to God. When you see truly happy people and you look into their eyes and see happiness, you see God within them. There is such a joy about them, a happiness that you long for. This is God. So put God in the center of your life, surrender to Him, and live in the present. By doing so, you will find that joy and happiness you are searching for.

Day 138

Do not let others dictate your joy. Let your joy come from within, from Me. Do not concern yourself with how they feel about you but how you feel about yourself.

> *The Lord your God is with you,*
> *the Mighty Warrior who saves.*
> *He will take great delight in you;*
> (Zephaniah 3:17 NIV)

Does your joy come from within? Are you too concerned with how others feel about you?

Day 139

I just want you to be happy. I want you to be happy and content with your life. Life is so glorious. Sometimes you forget to see and appreciate what is going on around you. Enjoy. Be.

> *I praise you because I am fearfully and wonderfully made;*
> *your works are wonderful,*
> *I know that full well.* (Psalm 139:14 NIV)

Are you happy and content with your life? Why or why not?

Day 140

Joy is a great word. It is happiness and contentment rolled into one. Learn about joy. Experience joy in your life. Be happy and content. It's a wonderful feeling.

> *Rejoice in the Lord always. I will say it again: Rejoice!* (Philippians 4:4 NIV)

What are three joys in your life you can rejoice in today?

Day 141

Joy. Not drama, not excitement—just joy. I will continue to bring much joy to your life. I will continue to bring much love and much happiness. You have learned how precious time is. You know how important it is to spend time with the important people in your life. Enjoy your life. Love your life. Keep space in your life to experience My joy.

> *The LORD has done it this very day;*
> *let us rejoice today and be glad.*
> (Psalm 118:24 NIV)

What are a few things God has done for you that make your heart glad?

Day 142

Experience joy. Experience the feeling of elation. Sometimes it is just for a second, and sometimes it is for a longer period of time. Feeling joy is the elevation of the soul. It lifts you up to Me. Joy is just the beginning of what heaven will be like all of the time. It is a glimpse. People can have joy in many things, such as in a blossoming flower or a chirping bird, or in the larger things such as the birth of a child or a marriage. Many things can bring joy. Take time today to notice not only your large joys but your small joys as well.

> *Though you have not seen him, you love him; and even though you do not see him now, you believe in him and are filled with an inexpressible and glorious joy, for you are receiving the end result of your faith, the salvation of your souls.*
> (1 Peter 1:8–9 NIV)

How can you begin to see and feel the joys that God blesses you with every day?

Day 143

Joy is happiness. Joy is being. Joy is being present. Today I want you to be joyous in the little things as well as in the big things.

> *I delight greatly in the* LORD*;*
> *my soul rejoices in my God.*
> *For he has clothed me with garments of salvation*
> *and arrayed me in a robe of his righteousness,*
> *as a bridegroom adorns his head like a priest,*
> *and as a bride adorns herself with her jewels.*
> (Isaiah 61:10 NIV)

God wants you to have joy every day. How will you work on this today?

Day 144

Find joy in the journey. That is what it's about. Find joy—and that joy is Me. Once you have found Me, you have found joy. Joy is such a beautiful word. Think about when you and I are as We. You feel such joy, peace, love, and happiness. When one of those feelings is in disarray, you do not have total joy; so, yes—life is about finding joy in the journey! All of this is possible, even during strife. Just come and walk with Me.

> *I have told you this so that my joy may be in you and that your joy may be complete.*
> (John 15:11 NIV)

Are you missing joy in your life? Do you understand that true joy is found with God? Pray to God today for this joy.

Day 145

Many people are going through life who are just not happy. They are so concerned with the future that they do not live in the present. They need to be present. Stop worrying and just be. This brings much happiness. Problems are just situations—situations that we can overcome together. Knowing that I am here to work with you to solve problems also leads to happiness.

> *Until now you have not asked for anything in my name. Ask and you will receive, and your joy will be complete.* (John 16:24 NIV)

What are a few situations that you have prayed to God about and He has answered? Do you know that God's joy is in you?

Day 146

Happiness is very difficult for some people to find. They continually look for it, but they look in the wrong places. It is through Me that people find happiness. Happiness is tied to so much: love, peacefulness, gratitude, and much more. The only true way to find this is by being with Me in My presence. Many people appear happy on the outside but are not truly happy. Those who find happiness have Me at the center of their lives. Begin to look at people who appear happy. Look to see if I am present in their eyes. If I am, there is true happiness. If I am not, you will see a hollowness; you will not see the smile reaching their eyes. Along with true happiness comes contentment. When you are truly happy, you are content. You are at peace with Me.

> *But blessed is the one who trusts in the LORD,*
> *whose confidence is in him.*
> *They will be like a tree planted by the water*
> *that sends out its roots by the stream.*
> *It does not fear when heat comes;*
> *its leaves are always green.*
> *It has no worries in a year of drought*
> *and never fails to bear fruit.*
> (Jeremiah 17:7–8 NIV)

Do you look for happiness in the wrong places? Do you understand that happiness is trusting God?

Day 147

Happiness and peace. Everyone is searching for these things. How do you find them? You find them through union with Me.

> *Yes, my soul, find rest in God;*
> *my hope comes from him.*
> (Psalm 62:5 NIV)

In what places outside of God have you looked for happiness and peace? Were they satisfying in the long run?

Day 148

Remember where happiness comes from—it comes from being with Me. Do not let outside circumstances affect you and your happiness. Do not let others dictate your happiness. Be careful of this. Keep on nourishing the inside, the heart, the soul. Do not let things on the outside take nutrition away from the inside. It will happen slowly at first and then more quickly. You won't even be aware of it until it is too late. You have worked so hard on your heart and your soul. Don't let the external break this down. It is a rough, hard road back. Don't veer off the highway. Turn around and come back to smoother roads.

> *Love the Lord your God with all your heart*
> *and with all your soul and with all your mind.*
> (Matthew 22:37 NIV)

Have you let your relationship with God slip away? How can you find your way back?

Day 149

Stress and anxiety will slowly cover happiness. You need to slowly chip away at the rock to rediscover the diamond inside you. Let's keep chipping away. I wish I could tell you that sometimes your happiness won't be squashed, but this is life. In eternity, however, I promise it won't ever be squashed! In the meantime, enjoy the life and the blessings you have! I wish for your happiness and joy.

> *But we are citizens of heaven. And we can hardly wait for a Savior from there. He is the Lord Jesus Christ. He has the power to bring everything under his control. By his power he will change our earthly bodies. They will become like his glorious body.* (Philippians 3:20–21)

Will you work with God to chip away the rock and find the diamond that God created inside of you?

CHAPTER 9

Blessings

See your blessings every day.

Blessings. We find blessings in everything when we choose to look for them. God gives us many blessings every day in nature. Take time to look out your window or take a walk and see God's blessings—whether it is the ladybug on the sidewalk, the hawk flying in the air, the dragonfly that flies right up to you, or the singing of the birds. These are God's blessings. God also gives you many more blessings—your significant other, your children, and your friends—many of the people in your life. Begin to see all of these people as your blessings from God. There are also blessings in strife. It often takes years to see the blessings in strife, but they are there. When looking at difficult situations, try to ask yourself, "What are the blessings in all of this?" God has given me many lessons on blessings. Some lessons may seem redundant, but this is evidence that we tend to take our blessings for granted.

Day 150

I love to bless My faithful ones. It is My faithful ones who actually see all of My blessings. Many people go through life not seeing their blessings. Many people just want more and more. It is always a shame for those who do not see their blessings, whether the blessings are small or big. This makes Me sad, but I understand. I just always hope that someday they will see all of the blessings they have received.

> *They sang to the Lord. They praised him. They gave thanks to him. They said, "The Lord is good. His faithful love to Israel continues forever."*
> (Ezra 3:11)

Do you see all of your blessings? The big blessings? The small blessings? Today, look for your blessings and praise God for His faithful love.

Day 151

I bless all of My children. The problem is that you might not see all of My blessings. You are so busy, so covered up, that you do not see or recognize the little things. I want you to become more aware of My blessings all day long. This will also help to build your faith.

> *The Lord bless you*
> *and keep you;*
> *the Lord make his face shine on you*
> *and be gracious to you;*
> *the Lord turn his face toward you*
> *and give you peace.* (Numbers 6:24–26 NIV)

Spend today looking at God's blessings in your life.

Day 152

Remember your blessings. Do not let your ego concentrate on the non-blessings. See your blessings every day.

> *Say to God, "What wonderful things you do!"*
> (Psalm 66:3)

See the wonderful things that God does for you today.

Day 153

I am so happy when you see all of your gifts—both big and small. I am so happy to do all of this for you. But what makes Me the happiest is that you know I have blessed you with these gifts. Never lose sight of this. You have so many wonderful gifts, yet many times you do not realize that all those things come from Me.

> *We are God's creation. He created us to belong to Christ Jesus. Now we can do good works. Long ago God prepared these works for us to do.* (Ephesians 2:10)

Do you thank God for your blessings and share your blessings through the works that you do?

Day 154

It is easy to look outside and see My blessings: the sky, clouds, birds, flowers, trees—and the list goes on. Look outside every day and see My blessings. This is just the tip of the iceberg. Your pets—what wonderful blessings! Your children—what amazing blessings! The trust and love that you give to them and that they give to you are wonderful. It is truly unconditional love. They are all blessings! The significant other in your life—what a blessing! Someone to spend your life with, to share your faith with—another blessing. Your friendships, those in your life, whether it is for a short moment or for a lifetime—what a blessing! There are so many blessings. Notice that I did not speak about material things. In the end, it is the beauty of nature and the people in your life that matter. Always remember that.

> *Every good and perfect gift is from God. This kind of gift comes down from the Father who created the heavenly lights. These lights create shadows that move. But the Father does not change like these shadows.* (James 1:17)

God has given you so many gifts. Make a list of them today.

Day 155

Blessings are a wonderful thing. There are blessings all around you every day. Some blessings are very simple; others are more elaborate. Some are as simple as butterflies, dragonflies, grasshoppers, the birds flying and singing, and the things of nature. Some are more elaborate, such as your children, your significant other, and your job. But they are all blessings nonetheless. Enjoy your blessings every day. Notice them. I have provided them for you.

> *Come and see what God has done.*
> *See what wonderful things*
> *he has done for people!* (Psalm 66:5)

Today, write down the names of all of the people God has blessed you with, and tell them that you love them.

Day 156

All of My children are blessed, but many do not see all of My blessings every day. I provide you with many blessings every day. There are insects, animals, flowers, mountains, and the sky—many blessings that My children do not witness and do not see daily. Starting with the smallest of blessings, begin to see them, recognize them, then move along and see other blessings, such as the people and situations in your life. The list goes on. Your blessings are always there; you just choose not to see them.

> *LORD, I will give thanks to you with all my heart.*
> *I will tell about all the wonderful things you have done.* (Psalm 9:1)

Can you commit to saying "Thank You" to God every day?

Day 157

There are always blessings in distress. These blessings are often not evident until after the distress has passed. This can often take weeks, months, or even years. So start searching for the blessings in your distress.

> *Give thanks no matter what happens.*
> *God wants you to thank him because you believe*
> *in Christ Jesus.* (1 Thessalonians 5:18)

Reflect on a stressful time in your life. Do you now see the blessings?

Day 158

It helps to look at blessings in every situation. Find a blessing in everything—both in good and bad situations. There is always a blessing. You can always ask Me, *God, what are the blessings of this? What am I to learn from this?* If you do, you will see it all in a different light.

> *About midnight Paul and Silas were praying and singing hymns to God, and the other prisoners were listening to them. Suddenly there was such a violent earthquake that the foundations of the prison were shaken. At once all the prison doors flew open, and everyone's chains came loose.*
> (Acts 16:25–26 NIV)

Reflect on a difficult situation. What did you learn from this situation? Do you now see that it was a blessing?

CHAPTER 10

Free Will

You are always in control of your actions.
Every day, every moment,
you make choices in your behavior.

God gave all of us freedom of choice, known as free will. We are free to choose God, and we are free not to choose Him. We are also given the freedom to make other choices. Some of our choices turn out well, and some of them do not. When they do not, we need to make sure that we are not blaming God or others for the choices that we made. These are our consequences. We need to understand that regardless of the choice that we have made, God still loves us and He will help us get through the consequences. God also loves it when we ask Him for guidance with our choices—both before and after. Who better to guide us than the One who loves us the most and will always look out for us?

Day 159

Every day is a good day. It just needs to be looked at as a good day. It is all a matter of perspective. Two people could be having the same day, and one person will say it was a great day while the other person will say it was a bad day. How you look at each moment of each day defines you. It makes up who you are. If you look at each moment as a gift, then the entire day is a blessing. Each moment just adds up to a great day. It is so easy to be happy and have good days by going from moment to moment and living in the present. This leads to much happiness. So if you are down or sad, just realize that each moment in time is a blessing. This mindset will really change not only that moment in time but also your entire day. This is part of just being.

My tongue will proclaim your righteousness,
your praises all day long. (Psalm 35:28 NIV)

How can you shift your perspective to begin taking each day moment by moment, all day long, and see these moments in a positive light?

Day 160

There are choices to be made every day, every moment of every life. Choice can define a person: good, bad, or indifferent. There are consequences with every choice. Human nature chooses the selfish option, the one that benefits the self most. Look at every decision you make. Try your best to make the one I would like you to make. Sometimes the choice is the one that is best for yourself, but most of the time it's the one that is best for someone else.

> *Let each of you look not only to his own interests,*
> *but also to the interests of others.*
> (Philippians 2:4 ESV)

Do you tend to make choices that are best for you or best for others?

Day 161

You make choices in life. Some people choose Me, and some people don't. Many people lead a good life and treat others well, and they have chosen Me. Others have not led a good life and have not treated others well, and they have not chosen Me. For those who have chosen Me, life is far easier. For those who have not chosen Me, life can be a difficult road. It is about choices. Humans have to live with their choices. I gave you free will. What you do with your free will is up to you.

> *I will guide you and teach you*
> *the way you should go.*
> *I will give you good advice*
> *and watch over you with love.* (Psalm 32:8)

What are some choices that you have made that you regret? How can you learn from these choices?

Day 162

It is human nature to take the easy way out. This is a product of society—the "me" society—doing what is best and easiest for "me." This has happened in history before, and it will happen again. It will also pass. You need to raise strong, responsible children. You need to do what is best for all and what is best for your fellow man.

> *Do not neglect to do good and to share what you have, for such sacrifices are pleasing to God.*
> (Hebrews 13:16 ESV)

What is an opportunity you have right now to do good for someone else?

Day 163

Sometimes you make a poor choice that can affect your entire life. When a poor choice is being made, there is a tug in your heart pulling you the other way; that is Me calling you to make the other choice. But you have free will, and you will need to live with the consequences of your actions. Sometimes these consequences are very difficult, but even then I am with you to help you get through. Surrender them to Me. Surrender your life—that is all I ask. Let Me help you make the right choices. Let Me help you find the right path.

> *If any of you needs wisdom, you should ask God for it. He will give it to you. God gives freely to everyone and doesn't find fault.* (James 1:5)

Have you ever consistently prayed that God would give you wisdom, especially regarding a decision you needed to make?

Day 164

People have free will. They make choices every day. Many people end up not liking the outcome of their choices, so they blame Me. *Why did God let this happen?* I did not let it happen. The choice was made—freedom of choice, free will. There are also the choices that people around you made. I did not make these choices either. Do not forget that I am not making the choices in your life; you are. If your choices do not turn out well, turn to Me and I will help you. Be with Me. Many people turn away from Me when things get bad. Turn *to* Me. I will help you. I do not want or wish for bad things to happen to My children, but sometimes they do. I will help My children get through the tough times.

> *The person who does what is right may have many troubles.*
> *But the Lord saves him from all of them.*
> (Psalm 34:19)

Do you blame God or do you turn toward Him after you make poor choices?

Day 165

Human will and freedom of choice are such great gifts, yet much tragedy can come from them. I gave you freedom of choice, and many use that freedom, yet they blame someone else or Me for their own choices. You will make wrong choices at times, and that is okay. I will be with you. But always speak to Me about the big choices. I will guide you in the correct way. I will lead you down the correct road.

> *Trust in the Lord with all your heart*
> *and lean not on your own understanding;*
> *in all your ways submit to him,*
> *and he will make your paths straight.*
> (Proverbs 3:5–6 NIV)

Do you take responsibility for your choices, or do you blame others—or even blame God?

Day 166

There are people who will make the choice not to be with Me. That is their choice, their free will. This saddens Me. However, I gave man free will. Some figure it out early in life. I need those to lead others. Some figure it out midlife. I also need those to help bring others home. For those who have figured it out, I need them to plant seeds and nourish them. Some seeds never sprout, but many others do. Plant seeds. Whether or not the seed sprouts is not up to you. It is their choice, and when they choose Me, I will make them grow. I need you to plant seeds for others by your words, your actions, and your choices.

> *So neither the one who plants nor the one who waters is anything, but only God, who makes things grow.* (1 Corinthians 3:7 NIV)

Are you willing to plant seeds of faith in other people's lives so that God is able to water them and make them grow?

Day 167

Let's discuss free choice. The most difficult part of free choice is that you can sometimes see the choices others are making, and when they appear to make the "bad choice," it is very difficult to watch. It can be heart-wrenching, but it is their choice to make this decision, not yours—and no matter what you do or how hard you try, you may or may not be able to change their decision. Their decisions are theirs and theirs alone. Therefore, the consequences of their actions are theirs and theirs alone. I know, though, that sometimes, many times, their choices affect others, and that can be the most difficult part. However, you can't do anything about it. Let it go. Can you help pick up the pieces? Sure you can, but ultimately, you cannot undo what they have done. You cannot undo the choice they have made. I know how difficult it is to watch. I see it all the time with My children. It is truly upsetting, but each person needs to grow and learn from their decisions. If they never make a poor decision, then they will never learn. If you don't let others make decisions and deal with the consequences, how will they learn?

> *The prayer of a righteous person is powerful and effective.* (James 5:16 NIV)

Who do you need to release to God's care? Will you pray for them, knowing that your prayers are powerful and effective?

Day 168

I am there to pick up the pieces for My children because of choices that others make. Freedom of choice is a wonderful thing that I blessed you with, but it also can cause much pain because many people do not use freedom of choice with love. They have created excuses and try to justify what they are doing, even when it is evil. Then, as a Father, I am there to pick up the pieces. It is painful to see My children cry. Know that I am here each and every day—loving you, holding you, and fixing you.

> *He heals the brokenhearted*
> *and binds up their wounds.*
> (Psalm 147:3 NIV)

What wounds have you incurred from other people's choices? Can you bring those hurts to God, allowing Him to bring you wholeness and healing?

CHAPTER 11

Truth

Remember that you do not have the entire truth.

Truth. Everyone believes that they have the entire truth. But in reality, you only have *your* truth—what you believe to be correct. Your truth is based on many things, including your upbringing, your morals, and your values. Two people can witness the same event and have different perceptions of the truth as to what happened. This is important to remember in your conversations with one another. When you realize that their perception of the truth is different from your perception of the truth, you will be able to come to a common ground with the other person and show them compassion. This realization will help you in all of your relationships.

Day 169

Life is so much easier when you are able to empathize with one another and realize that most people do not intentionally hurt one another. It is so easy for your ego to get in the way. Most people believe they are being fair, even when you explain your view to them and they are steadfast in what they believe. Remember that you do not have their perception or their viewpoint, and since you don't, you might believe they are being unfair. This is true in any disagreement. Always try to remember that you only have your own perception of the truth. Each person's perception is different based on many things, such as environment, upbringing, viewpoint, emotions at the time, and circumstances. You can be at the same place at the same time, but both people view the same thing differently because you are different people with different experiences, different perspectives, and different emotions.

> *Let us consider how we can stir up one another to love. Let us help one another to do good works.*
> (Hebrews 10:24)

Instead of stirring up one another to anger, how can you use empathy to understand another's perception and love today?

Day 170

During disagreements, your ego is at its largest. This adds even more difficulty to overcoming the disagreement. All reasoning from the heart goes out the window. Your ego becomes angry because you are unable to see another's point of view and that other person cannot see yours. So where does it end? It ends with realizing that you both have separate perceptions of the truth and that you both love each other and do not want to hurt each other. Understand that they might not realize what they are doing—or that you might not realize what you are doing. Come from a place of the heart rather than from the ego.

> *Those of us who are strong and able in the faith need to step in and lend a hand to those who falter, and not just do what is most convenient for us. Strength is for service, not status. Each one of us needs to look after the good of the people around us, asking ourselves, "How can I help?"*
> (Romans 15:1–2 MSG)

Are you in conflict with anyone in your life right now? What if you stopped, started over by coming from a place of your heart, and understood that you do not know their perception of the truth?

Day 171

Treat everyone with love and kindness. Take it one step further when telling your perception of the truth about a situation: do it with love and kindness. You will see that you get much further in a conversation. Instead of putting someone on the defensive, you put them at ease. You show them love and kindness. Again, speak your perception of the truth, but be loving and kind. People appreciate knowing your perception, but even more, they appreciate the love and kindness.

> *Instead, speaking the truth in love, we will grow to become in every respect the mature body of him who is the head, that is, Christ.*
> (Ephesians 4:15 NIV)

How can you begin to train yourself to speak your perception of the truth with love and kindness?

CHAPTER 12

Trust

Once you can trust Me fully,
life becomes more peaceful and worry-free.

God wants us to trust in Him. Trust Him in all aspects of your life, both big and small. Trust builds faith. When you reach this level of trust, you find peacefulness with Him.

Day 172

Trust in Me is paramount. Once you can trust Me fully, life becomes more peaceful and worry free, but it takes much faith. As you begin to trust in Me, your faith will grow. Every time you trust in Me and it works out, your faith grows. It is like a flower that has a bud. Inside that bud, faith is growing. As the flower begins to open up, faith and trust are continuing to grow and develop. Soon you have a glorious bloom—glorious faith and trust. Continue to trust in Me, and you will have an entire meadow of blooming, glorious flowers. That is faith and trust. Then you will have complete peacefulness.

> *LORD, those who know you will trust in you.*
> *You have never deserted those*
> *who look to you.* (Psalm 9:10)

Are you seeing your faith grow as you trust God? Do you want to have an entire meadow of faith?

Day 173

Truly trusting Me in all aspects of your life is very difficult. There are very few people who have been able to do this. Mother Teresa is one of them. Her faith and trust in Me were truly amazing. She completely turned her life over to Me. I am not asking that you do this—to be on her journey. I am asking that you do turn your life over to Me and trust in Me. Be more present every day. Do not let your mind take you far from Me. Let go and trust in Me. Live from your heart and be present.

> *Jesus Christ is the same yesterday and today and forever.* (Hebrews 13:9 NIV)

Why is it sometimes easier to trust people, who are constantly changing, than it is to trust our God, who remains the same?

Day 174

Everyone has cracks; some cracks are just bigger than others. Trust in Me to smooth out your cracks and make them disappear. Trust that when we discover a crack, we will work on it together. Trust that I will mend or glue the crack so it will stop getting bigger. Just as with a fine piece of porcelain, there will always be fissures. These cracks add to the beauty of the piece. When a crack begins, it is up to the owner of the piece to bring it to Me for repair. If the owner chooses not to bring it in for repair, then the piece is thrown away and never fixed. With Me, no piece is beyond repair. Regardless of how damaged the piece is, if the owner comes to Me, we can work together and repair it.

> *Lord, people find the will to live because you keep your promises.*
> *And my spirit also finds life in your promises.*
> *You brought me back to health.*
> *You let me live.*
> *I'm sure it was for my benefit*
> *that I suffered such great pain.*
> *You love me. You kept me*
> *from going down into the pit of death.*
> (Isaiah 38:16–17)

What are the cracks that you are suffering from right now? Do you trust that God can mend those cracks back to health?

Day 175

Trust goes further than trusting Me. You also need to trust yourself. Trust yourself to do the right thing. Trust yourself to trust Me. Think about that—trust yourself to trust Me. You know you want to trust Me, for that is the foundation of faith, but go one step further and trust yourself to do that.

> *Don't let your hearts be troubled. Trust in God, and trust also in me.* (John 14:1 NLT)

Do you trust yourself to trust God?

CHAPTER 13

Wisdom

Wisdom is of the heart.

Wisdom comes from God. Many people confuse wisdom with intelligence. Intelligence is of the mind, but wisdom is of the heart. How do you know the difference? If it is of the heart, it is of love, kindness, joy, peace, and everything that is of God. If you act on what you believe is wisdom and it is not of God, such as anger, hate, greed, or any other negativity, then that is not wisdom. That is "ego wisdom." When it comes from the heart, it is "God wisdom."

Day 176

Wisdom is something that everyone can have. You need to be open to it like everything else I teach. Educate yourself and listen to Me about wisdom. Learn your faith. Read. Listen and speak to others. Through this, you will gain wisdom. Be open to what I say. Listen and learn. Apply what you have learned, and you will have wisdom.

> *The LORD gives wisdom.*
> *Knowledge and understanding*
> *come from his mouth.* (Proverbs 2:6)

Are you open to learning God's wisdom?

Day 177

When you rise early to be with Me, you are empty. You are emptier than you are the rest of the day. Before the day begins to fill up, it is so much easier for you to hear Me and for Me to fill you with wisdom. You are not rushed. All is quiet, and it's just you and Me. It is truly a wonderful, magical quiet time early in the morning before the world awakens. Why do you think I wake you up early? I am so excited to speak with you that I have a childlike excitement. Just as you look forward to this time, so do I. Just as you are excited to see your children, I am excited to see you, for we are a parent and child seeing and visiting each other and spending quality time together. It is truly beautiful and glorious.

> *He who rises early to seek her will have no difficulty, for he will find her sitting at his gates.*
> (Wisdom of Solomon 6:14 RSV)

Will you begin a routine of waking up early to spend time with God?

Day 178

There are many types of wisdom. I gave the apostles wisdom to understand Scripture. This wisdom is very special. I still grant this type of wisdom to many people. Then there is wisdom in the knowledge of Me. I have also granted this to many people. There is also wisdom granted in various situations. I grant this all of the time. Many people pray for this type of wisdom—wisdom in handling a situation about work or friendship or family the way I want you to handle them—with love!

> *Don't fool yourselves. Suppose some of you think you are wise by the standards of the world. Then you should become "fools" so that you can become wise.* (1 Corinthians 3:18)

There is worldly wisdom and there is godly wisdom; which do you rely on more?

Day 179

When you ask for wisdom, you are asking Me to help you in a situation. You are asking for My opinion. There might be times when you think you are using My wisdom but your ego is in the way instead. Decisions are being based on your ego and not on wisdom. How do you know the difference? If the words are kind and loving, if the action is ethical, and if you are in My teachings, you are in My wisdom—God's wisdom. However, if there is anger, hurt, greed, and unethical behavior, that comes from ego wisdom. Learn the difference. It will make life so much easier.

> *Is anyone among you wise and understanding? That person should show it by living a good life. A wise person isn't proud when they do good deeds.* (James 3:13)

What type of wisdom do you use? Is it God-based or ego-based? How do you know the difference?

Day 180

Wisdom is really knowing the right thing to do. It becomes clouded by your ego and mind. It is an oxymoron because people believe that wisdom is of the mind, but it is really of the heart. The mind gets in the way of true wisdom. Remember that wisdom is different from intelligence. Intelligence is of the mind, but intelligence tries to take over wisdom. Wisdom asks what is in the best interest of each person involved. Wisdom is not having to win and get your own way. It is truly what is in the best interest of others. It comes from Me.

> *Wisdom and power belong to God.*
> *Advice and understanding also belong to him.*
> (Job 12:13)

Has there been a time in your life when your intelligence has conflicted with your wisdom? What choice did you make?

CHAPTER 14

Space and Time

Space is necessary for Me.

Space is necessary for God. Do you have enough space for God? Many people are so busy in their lives that they actually do not have the space for Him. All God wants is for us to find space and have time for Him—to allow Him to work within you, to allow Him to be with you. Remember that it is your choice to be with Him, for He gave you freedom of choice. What does your day look like? Do you tend to schedule every minute of every day? If you do, then there is no way that you have space for God or for anyone else in your life. Time goes by so quickly, and God wants you to enjoy all of the blessings He has given to you. He wants you to enjoy your loved ones and your family. People today waste so much time worrying about the future. God wants you to be present with Him.

Day 181

Space is necessary for Me. When you take up space with many things, you squash space for Me. When things are taking up your space, ask yourself if it is worth using up this space that you should have for Me.

> *It was very early in the morning and still dark. Jesus got up and left the house. He went to a place where he could be alone. There he prayed.*
> (Mark 1:35)

If Jesus took time to make space for God, how important is it for us to do the same?

Day 182

When your burdens are taking up too much space, breathe in the Holy Spirit, and then release the burdens to Me. Picture the Holy Spirit being breathed in and your thoughts being breathed out. The Holy Spirit is your oxygen, and the "waste" is your carbon dioxide.

> *May the God who gives hope fill you with great joy. May you have perfect peace as you trust in him. May the power of the Holy Spirit fill you with hope.* (Romans 15:13)

Can you relieve yourself from your burdens by breathing in the Holy Spirit and releasing them to receive hope and joy?

Day 183

When you make space for Me, our relationship becomes stronger. The more space you give Me, the more room I have to work within you. When you surrender a situation to Me, I have more power to help guide you. Do you see this? As you take out the garbage in your life, you leave more space for Me. My vessel within you becomes larger and more spacious and is filled with more and more of Me. This becomes evident in all you do and in who you are.

> *I have been crucified with Christ. I don't live any longer, but Christ lives in me. Now I live my life in my body by faith in the Son of God. He loved me and gave himself for me.* (Galatians 2:20)

How can you decrease so that God can increase?

Day 184

No one is whole without Me. When your space is so taken up by things of the earth and not by Me, you are not whole. You are missing the key ingredient. It is like making a cake without the flour. The cake is flat. It is not airy. This is you without Me. You are flat and not airy, but just heavy. However, when there is flour, just the opposite happens. It is light and airy. How can you be joyful and at peace if you are searching to complete yourself? Sometimes people fill themselves with the negative things of the world, but when you fill yourself with Me, the search is over and there is peace, happiness, and love—and that is beautiful!

> *Jesus saith unto him,*
> *Rise, take up thy bed, and walk.*
> *And immediately the man was made whole, and*
> *took up his bed, and walked.* (John 5:8–9 KJV)

God wants us to be whole. What do you need to take up—to get rid of—in order for God to fill you?

Day 185

You have packed your days too full. Take a step back and slow down. There is no need to fill up every minute of your day. Many things can wait. Let them wait. When you fill up your day so full, you do not have space for Me. Take time today to be with Me. This will make your day less busy and less stressful. Relax.

> *The LORD is good to those whose hope is in him,*
> *to the one who seeks him.*
> (Lamentations 3:25 NIV)

Will you take time today to seek God?

Day 186

I feel that we are getting closer and closer. This makes Me very happy. You are calling to Me throughout the day. I know that things of the world will try to sneak in, but let's make sure that does not happen. How? Run into your fortified house and shut the door. You have some peace right now. It is time to use it to patch the roof after the last storm and make it stronger. How? By being together. Take a walk outside and walk with Me for just ten minutes. This time will help to keep your space for Me. When you feel your space being gobbled up, take time with Me.

> *The Lord has told you what is good,*
> *and this is what he requires of you:*
> *to do what is right, to love mercy,*
> *and to walk humbly with your God.*
> (Micah 6:8 NLT)

If you were able to take a walk with God today, how did it feel to simply just be in His presence? If you were not able, how can you begin to schedule a daily ten-minute walk with God?

Day 187

The thief takes your space a little at a time—so little that you do not notice—and then suddenly so much is gone. That is how it happens. How easy it is to take your space and fill it! Your space needs to be filled with Me and nothing else. How? When your brain gets too busy, speak to Me. Look around you and see My beauty. Don't let that brain start creating new problems. Take a deep breath and, if possible, take a walk and refocus on Me.

> *But seek first his kingdom and his righteousness,*
> *and all these things will be given to you.*
> (Matthew 6:33 NIV)

Is the thief stealing your space for God? What or who is the thief in your life? How can you seek God first?

Day 188

We have spoken about freedom of choice. Let's discuss it regarding space. Space is very important for you to have, for without space, there is no room for Me! Every day, though, you make choices to fill up your space. You fill it up with things that do not matter, things you have zero control over. These are important choices. Say, *God, please do not let these things take up my space. Help me to release them to You.* Take a deep breath and let it go. Feel it leaving your body, and breathe Me in. This will work. Practice this breathing exercise, and pray to Me to take these other things away.

> *Lord, heal me. Then I will be healed.*
> *Save me from my enemies.*
> *Then I will be saved.*
> *You are the one I praise.* (Jeremiah 17:14)

If God is capable of healing and saving us, don't you think that He is also capable of carrying our burdens? How can you release your worries and cares to Him today?

Day 189

Time is something that you don't get back. Time is precious. Spend time with family and friends. Make time for loved ones. Make time for Me. Many people worry about time, but when you live in the present, you won't worry as much about time.

> *For he says, "In the time of my favor I heard you, and in the day of salvation I helped you." I tell you, now is the time of God's favor, now is the day of salvation.* (2 Corinthians 6:2 NIV)

Find time this week for family, friends, and, most of all, for God.

Day 190

Relationships with family, your children, your significant other, your friends, and Me take time. Sometimes you can't always do all you want because of lack of time. Learn to give some things up to make time for these important people and for Me.

> *Dear friends, let us love one another, for love comes from God. Everyone who loves has been born of God and knows God.* (1 John 4:7 NIV)

We show others that we love them by making time for them. Who do you need to make more time for right now?

Day 191

Do you see how important and precious time is? Time is something you never get back. Treasure your time with Me and with those you love. Money is not worth it. There needs to be a balance between money and time.

> *Your heart will be where your riches are.*
> (Matthew 6:21)

If someone were to gauge where your heart is based upon how important money is to you, what would they see?

Day 192

How important it is to have time for the important things in life! Are you too worried about finances? Do you have all you need? No more, no less? I will make sure you have what you need. Trust in Me. Keep your faith in Me. I am the one who will take care of you. You tend to get caught up in the little things, in the things that don't matter. Appreciate and make time for the things that do matter. Don't lose sight of them. They are what life is about—your significant other, your children, your family, and your friends. You are truly blessed. Enjoy your life. Enjoy your blessings.

> *Anyone who loves money never has enough.*
> *Anyone who loves wealth is never satisfied*
> *with what they get.*
> *That doesn't have any meaning either.*
> (Ecclesiastes 5:10)

What role does money play in your everyday attitude?

Day 193

Time is so precious. Don't waste it worrying about something that may or may not happen. Just let it go. I will take care of it. I will take care of you. It will be okay. Let it go.

> *But I know that God helps me.*
> *The Lord is the one who keeps me going.*
> (Psalm 54:4)

Do you have a burden that is consuming your time? Will you allow God to help you?

Day 194

Time does go fast. There are times when it seems to go slowly, but when you look back, it has so quickly gone. Life on Earth is just a flash of time. Look back at a difficult time in your life. It is just a flash. Don't let that difficult time cause you so much pain. It's not worth it. At some point when you look back, it will be a distant memory—almost like it did not happen. It will seem like just a brief flash in time. Memories will fade, and the hurt and pain will fade too.

> *All people are like grass.*
> *All their glory is like the flowers in the field.*
> *The grass dries up. The flowers fall to the ground.*
> (1 Peter 1:24)

How does being reminded that our time on Earth is temporary make you feel about the importance of the burdens that are concerning you right now?

Day 195

Time does go fast. Look how quickly the last month has gone by. Then look at the years, and then look at your entire life. Time does move quickly, and what do you learn from this? Make the most of every moment, every day, every month, and every year, for it will pass by very quickly. You tend to forget this as you go through the daily grind of life. Every day, every moment, is a blessing. Use the most of it.

> *Those who use the things of the world should not become all wrapped up in them. The world as it now exists is passing away.* (1 Corinthians 7:31)

When you look back at the last month, do you see how quickly it went by? What about the last year? The last five years? Your entire life? When you look at it this way, do you see the importance of spending it with loved ones and with God?

Day 196

Time is something that everyone has. Some seem to have too much, while others seem not to have enough. It is so easy to fill it up, and yet so difficult to empty it out. It is most difficult to have the time for Me. There is so much going on. Many people wish they had more time, and then when they do, they do not know what to do with it. When you feel as if you are wasting time, sitting with "nothing" to do, you are actually spending time wisely. You are being restored, revitalizing yourself. This is far from wasting time. Yet when you are busy, you are actually wasting your time. Have you ever had every minute of the day planned? How stressful was that? That behavior is not healthy, and it leaves no time, no space, for Me. The mind is always reeling with what needs to be done.

> *Dear friends, here is one thing you must not forget. With the Lord a day is like a thousand years. And a thousand years are like a day.*
> (2 Peter 3:8)

What is your attitude toward time? What do you think God's attitude is toward time?

Day 197

Life often seems to move slowly during times of strife. That is a result of being caught up in the strife. When life is peaceful and happy, time seems to move much more quickly. Why is this? This is because when you are enjoying your life, it appears to fly by, but when you are in times of strife, you are concentrating on the negative. This tends to drag you down and make you tired, so time seems to move more slowly. I want your weeks to fly by in joy, not move more slowly during difficult times. Life should be enjoyed. Life should be happy. Life should be joyous. It is like walking through the water. When it is clear and calm, you can go right through. You are looking at everything with awe and wonder—the fish, plants, shells, etc. But walking through muddy, thick waters seems to take forever. Time goes slowly. It is miserable, so walk through the clear waters and not the muddy waters. This way you can concentrate on My beauty.

> *Finally, my brothers and sisters, always think about what is true. Think about what is noble, right and pure. Think about what is lovely and worthy of respect. If anything is excellent or worthy of praise, think about those kinds of things.* (Philippians 4:8)

How can you shift your thinking to concentrate on God's beauty? On things that are noble, right, and pure? On the things of God?

Day 198

I gave humans a mind to help them to survive, not to push Me away. Society has become very busy. People don't slow down. There is always more to do. To sit down and relax has become a luxury that people don't indulge in. The problem is that there is no room for Me—so you need to clear your mind. One way to do this is through writing. Write down everything on your mind, mark your worries, and surrender them to Me. This will help you to have more space. You will be surprised how much of your mind is taken up by worries. Worrying is a waste of time and space. Only I know the future. So acknowledge your worries, surrender them, and clear up some space for Me.

> *I was very worried.*
> *But your comfort brought me joy.*
> (Psalm 94:19)

Take a few minutes right now to write out your thoughts. Put a check mark beside all the thoughts that are your worries. Can you give those to God? Can you exchange your anxiety for His joy?

CHAPTER 15

Patience shows total trust in Me.

Patience. Why is it so difficult to be patient? It is difficult mainly because we are not living in the present with God. If we fully trusted in Him, we would truly believe that He would take care of and provide for us, like birds that never worry where their next meal is coming from. Patience gives us freedom—freedom to be in the present and to trust in God. Why is this so hard? It is difficult because we fill every day to the brim and are so busy that we forget what is important—loving God and loving our neighbor. We have become a "me" society. We are impatient to receive things, and we are impatient for the future. We forget to live in the present with God. We need to surrender and trust in Him. When we do this, our patience with ourselves and others will multiply. So be in the present, in His presence, and have patience!

Day 199

Continue to have patience and trust in Me. I will lead you down the correct path. Remember that things happen in My time and not in yours. It is easier to understand this concept than it is to practice it. Patience shows total trust in Me. This can be very difficult because it means turning your life over to Me and trusting Me with your future. Remember that the future is My worry and not yours. Be patient. Then, after patience, comes the trust that I will make everything work out.

> *We hope for what we don't have yet. So we are patient as we wait for it.* (Romans 8:25)

Are you willing to have patience with God's plan in your life? Are you willing to trust that His plan is what is best for you?

Day 200

Having patience is difficult. Surrendering all things to Me makes patience easier. Just knowing that I will take care of you and all aspects of your life will also make it easier. Patience is often difficult because you are not living in the present. You are impatient because you are waiting for something in the future. Be happy in the present, in My presence, and patience will be obtained.

> *Rejoice in hope, be patient in tribulation, be constant in prayer.* (Romans 12:12 ESV)

Do you know that patience is made easier by surrendering your life to God?

Day 201

Be patient. Be kind. Let them see Me in you. Take these words seriously. Live in the present. If you are living in the present, patience is easy. It is the future things that you pursue that make you impatient. Be present. Be patient. Be kind. Be kind in every situation. Kindness is extremely important in letting people see Me in you. Being kind can change someone's day. Be patient and kind today. Most importantly, be present. Doing so will let others see Me in you.

> *You are the light of the world. A town built on a hill cannot be hidden. Neither do people light a lamp and put it under a bowl. Instead they put it on its stand, and it gives light to everyone in the house. In the same way, let your light shine before others, that they may see your good deeds and glorify your Father in heaven.*
> (Matthew 5:14–16 NIV)

Are you a light by showing kindness in the world? Does your light shine before others, reflecting the light of God from within?

Day 202

It can be very difficult to be patient. In today's society, people want everything now. People are not used to waiting. People do not like when they have to wait. Having patience is a gift. You need to teach your children to have patience. They are being raised to get everything right away. This is a problem. This is why many people have debt. It is okay to wait for things. It makes you appreciate them much more.

> *Start children off on the right path.*
> *And even when they are old,*
> *they will not turn away from it.* (Proverbs 22:6)

Are you raising children who are impatient and need things right away, or are you teaching them patience?

Day 203

Patience. I talk a lot about patience. Patience is difficult for the human spirit. In today's world, people are going, going, going. It is a very "me now" society. People want something, and they want it now. It has become very difficult to be patient.

> *But if we hope for what we do not see, we wait for it with patience.* (Romans 8:25 ESV)

What is it most difficult for you to wait for with patience?

Day 204

It can be very difficult to be patient, but it is very important to have patience. How can you love your neighbor if you are not being patient? Often when you are not being patient with someone, it is because you do not understand their story. You do not know what is going on in their life. Step back, take a breath, and have patience. Know that it is My child you are being impatient with. Show that person love. When you are being impatient, you are not showing My love. Think of that person as Me. Show them love, and then patience will come much easier.

> *Love is patient. Love is kind. It does not want what belongs to others. It does not brag. It is not proud.* (1 Corinthians 13:4)

Have you ever shown someone love and patience when they were being difficult? What was that like? What was the result?

Day 205

Have patience. Sometimes it is very difficult to be patient, especially when your patience is being tested. It is then that it is most important to show patience. Those are the times I really want you to concentrate.

> *Let us not become tired of doing good. At the right time we will gather a crop if we don't give up.*
> (Galatians 6:9)

Do you ever get tired of being patient with certain people? From what you are learning about patience, how can you work on this?

Day 206

Being patient is very difficult, especially when you feel there are situations in your life that are up in the air. Not only do you have to have patience, but you have to have faith and trust in Me. Patience—when will it happen? It will happen in My time. My timing is perfect. My planning for you is perfect. You will need to be present and trust Me about your future. Yes, it all ties together. Faith, trust, patience, present, My presence, peace, love, understanding—they all tie together. Everything is intertwined. Do your best to master one at a time; then you will have union with Me.

> *The end of a matter is better than its beginning.*
> *So it's better to be patient than proud.*
> (Ecclesiastes 7:8)

Does worry of future events cause you to be impatient?

Day 207

Patience is twofold. First, be patient for the things to come. Second, be patient with others. Remember these two parts.

> *Put on then, as God's chosen ones, holy and beloved, compassionate hearts, kindness, humility, meekness, and patience.* (Colossians 3:12 ESV)

Do you understand that God wants you to have patience with others? How can you be better at this?

Day 208

When you feel anger or impatience, cry out to Me and ask Me for help. Ask Me for patience. Ask Me to suppress your anger. Let Me help you release the anger from your body. When your patience runs short, remember to call to Me and ask for help. I will give you the patience that you need.

> *But those who trust in the* LORD
> *will receive new strength.*
> *They will fly as high as eagles.*
> *They will run and not get tired.*
> *They will walk and not grow weak.*
> (Isaiah 40:31)

Have you ever cried out to God for patience or for help to suppress your anger? Did it work?

Day 209

Be patient. Be kind. Love is the basis of life. Many people know this, but they forget to also be patient and kind. Having both of these qualities truly shows your love. You cannot have true love without patience and kindness.

> *But the fruit of the Spirit is love, joy, peace, patience, kindness, goodness, faithfulness, gentleness, self-control.* (Galatians 5:22–23 ESV)

Patience, love, and kindness go hand in hand. Which do you need to work on?

CHAPTER 16

Kindness lets others see Me in you.

Kindness to others is something that God wants from us each day. God understands that sometimes it is much easier for us to be angry and bothered by others than it is to be kind. Kindness shows strength. Many people in our society believe that kindness shows weakness. God continually tells us that kindness is strength. He wants us to be kind, not only to those to whom it is easy to be kind, but also to those to whom it is difficult. It is wonderful to see a transformation right in front of us when we are kind to those who are difficult. We do not know what is going on in other people's lives and what difficulties they may be facing. We are all human, and sometimes we just need a word of kindness from another human being. We just need to feel the love. Through kindness, others are able to see God within you.

Day 210

Just be kind. Kindness often goes a long way. Being kind can change a person's day and a person's attitude. As the saying goes, you can "kill them with kindness." Be kind to all with whom you come in contact. Since you never know someone's story, an act of kindness might change their day and even their situation. That is why I always tell you to be kind.

> *Don't let any evil talk come out of your mouths. Say only what will help to build others up and meet their needs. Then what you say will help those who listen.* (Ephesians 4:29)

Has someone else's kindness ever helped you in a time of need? How can you pay it forward and do the same for someone else?

Day 211

Do not lose sight of being kind. Be kind to one another. Be kind, be loving, and be respectful. Treat everyone as My child, and know that I love them as much as I love you.

> *He has done it to show the riches of his grace for all time to come. His grace can't be compared with anything else. He has shown it by being kind to us. He was kind to us because of what Christ Jesus has done.* (Ephesians 2:7)

Are you kind, loving, and respectful to others?

Day 212

When you are kind to someone, amazing things happen. It lifts you up as well. If someone is being judgmental, point out something positive about the other person. It is amazing what will happen. The person will stop being judgmental—or you can point out that you do not know what this person is struggling with in their life and that it is not really fair to speak negatively about them. This, too, will "nip it in the bud." I am the only one who has the right to judge someone's heart. I am the only one who knows what is happening in that person's life. You do not. To judge another person's motivation shows ignorance. It is much better to lift someone up than to pull them down. Those acts of kindness often go a long way. There is much joy in lifting up another human being. It makes Me so happy.

> *Do not judge other people.*
> *Then you will not be judged.* (Matthew 7:1)

When others around you are being judgmental, how can you steer the conversation in a positive direction?

Day 213

Kindness is difficult for many people. Treating your fellow man with kindness is important. You never quite know what someone is going through, and just a small act of kindness can change someone's day or life. Being kind also helps people put some faith in mankind. So many things can be changed with kindness. Be kind.

> *The native people showed an unusual kindness,*
> *for they kindled a fire and welcomed us all,*
> *because it had begun to rain and was cold.*
> (Acts 28:2 ESV)

In what ways can you begin showing kindness to everyone you meet?

Day 214

Just be kind. You never know what another person is going through or why they are acting the way they are.

> *Let brotherly love continue. Do not neglect to show hospitality to strangers, for thereby some have entertained angels unawares.*
> (Hebrews 13:1–2 ESV)

Was there a time when you did not show kindness to someone and you regretted it later?

Day 215

Kindness goes a long way in helping people. When they see you being kind, even to those who irritate you, they see Me in you. Be kind every day. It is a simple act, but it is very important in your life. It is important to others as well. It is important to Me. So be kind. Be kind to your enemies. Be kind to those who are difficult. You can often change a situation with kindness. It is fun to see the transformation of someone's personality when you show kindness. So just be kind.

> *Suppose someone slaps you on your right cheek.*
> *Turn your other cheek to them also.*
> (Matthew 5:39)

Try being kind to those who irritate you or are being difficult. How does that make you feel? How does that change the situation?

Day 216

Be kind. Kindness lets others see Me in you. It is such a small thing, but the act of kindness is huge. You continually see the acknowledgment on people's faces every day when you are kind—especially on the faces of total strangers.

> *Whoever pursues righteousness and kindness will find life, righteousness, and honor.*
> (Proverbs 21:21 ESV)

Do you want others to see God in you? Do you want them to see His love through your compassion and kindness?

Day 217

Being kind means so much to Me. It makes Me smile when I see you being extra kind. It makes Me so proud of you. You will encounter many of My children who are difficult or different; you need to work on being kind to these people especially. It is easy to be kind to those who are already nice. It is more difficult to be kind to those who are difficult or different, but the impact of your kindness can totally change these people.

> *In everything, do to others what you would want them to do to you.* (Matthew 7:12)

When you are struggling or being difficult, do you want others to treat you with kindness? If so, then shouldn't you treat those who are struggling or being difficult in the same way that you want to be treated?

Day 218

There is much to learn about kindness. Yes, it is true that others perceive kindness as weakness, yet many times it is harder to be kind than not. It is tougher to put aside the ego and to be in the heart and be kind. This is true strength. I know that the pull to the ego and anger is strong, but let the pull of your heart win. It is the tug-of-war. It appears as if the strength is on the ego side, but the heart is a big muscle—the strongest in the body. Develop your heart and let it get stronger and stronger. Soon it will overpower the ego. To love from the heart is true strength. When you do, the ego will weaken because you are not exercising it. The ego will atrophy. However, many people work out the ego so much that it becomes stronger than the heart, and then their heart atrophies. Work out your heart. Let this muscle become so strong that it pulls the rope with more strength than the ego. Keep your heart strong.

> *Love one another deeply. Honor others more than yourselves.* (Romans 12:10)

Are you working out your heart or your ego? Are you strengthening your heart by loving deeply?

Day 219

I greatly appreciate it when My children help others. I appreciate it and I see it. Good deeds never go unnoticed by Me!

> *Finally, I want all of you to agree with one another. Be understanding. Love one another. Be kind and tender. Be humble.* (1 Peter 3:8)

Do you realize that God notices all good deeds?

CHAPTER 17

The Heart

I am present in your heart and in your soul.

God is present in your heart. The heart represents love, and God is love. Many of us live from our minds. The mind is a wonderful tool to help us in life, but the heart is where we find love. It is where we find God. God wants us to live from our hearts.

Day 220

The heart is a beautiful organ, not just in its anatomy, but in its physiological function. You need to live from your heart. The mind is also a wonderful part of the body, but it can get in the way of your heart. You need to love and come to Me through your heart. If your brain/mind starts to take over, then you will not believe. The mind tells you that I cannot be speaking to you right now. However, the heart tells you it is so. I am present in your heart and in your soul. This is how I made you. When you need Me, ask for Me with your heart. I am with you through your heart like the blood pulsing through your body. It is the heart that keeps you alive; without the heart, you would die. It is the same with Me. I keep you alive. I am coursing through your body, just like your blood. I am the life within you. This is why I chose the heart and not the mind. Close off the mind. Use your heart.

> *As water reflects the face,*
> *so one's life reflects the heart.*
> (Proverbs 27:19 NIV)

Does your mind get in the way of your relationship with God?

Day 221

I think it helps to make clear the difference between the heart and the mind. It is funny how the heart has been chosen as the symbol of love, because that is what I am—love. You see hearts on Valentine's Day. You see hearts when someone loves you. This is also where I am—in the heart, where love resides—not in the mind, which is busy analyzing situations. When you feel love, you feel it from the heart rather than from the mind. That is the same with Me. You love Me with your heart. I love you through your heart. No matter how the mind tries to analyze things to tell you that My love for you is not true, do not listen to the mind. Listen to your heart.

> *You shall love the Lord your God with all your heart and with all your soul and with all your strength and with all your mind, and your neighbor as yourself.* (Luke 10:27 ESV)

Do you feel God's love in your heart?

Day 222

The heart. All good resides in the heart. It begins with the heart. This is where I am. Somehow people have gotten away from the heart. That makes Me sad. I am the heart. Keep Me in your heart. Be aware of Me in your heart. Love Me from your heart.

> *Create in me a pure heart, O God,*
> *and renew a steadfast spirit within me.*
> (Psalm 51:10 NIV)

Are you more mind-based or heart-based?

Day 223

Do you see friends with "holes in their hearts"? Do you see them searching? When they are searching and are not fulfilled or feeling whole, it is because they are searching for Me. They will not find true peace until they find Me. They are filling this hole with alcohol, sex, gifts, purchases, or whatever habit they have. They will not be able to be at peace until they fill that hole with Me. Then their need for these things will subside. It is like a man in the desert searching for water. He will not quench his thirst until he finds water. Your friends may not believe you if you tell them that it is Me they are searching for, but if they truly wish to change or find what they are searching for, they might come to you for guidance. Will they ever come? I hope so. I want all of My children to find their way home to Me, and I am happy when they do.

> *Take delight in the* L*ORD*,
> *and he will give you the desires of your heart.*
> (Psalm 37:4 NIV)

Have you been searching and filling your void with negative habits? Do you see that it is God you have been searching for?

Day 224

Be in your heart. Be in your heart always. The mind is for keeping you safe, figuring numbers, and things like that. It is not for love. Love is in the heart. Love from your heart, not your mind.

> *Let love and faithfulness never leave you;*
> *bind them around your neck,*
> *write them on the tablet of your heart.*
> *Then you will win favor and a good name*
> *in the sight of God and man.*
> (Proverbs 3:3–4 NIV)

Are you willing to live from your heart? How can you accomplish this?

Day 225

Those whose hearts have been covered by greed, hate, dislike, money, gossip, and judgmentalism are hard to reach. My light has been covered. What can you do? You can treat them with kindness. Many people are always on the verge of lashing out and will use anything as an opportunity to do this. So be kind and generous with them. Remember that it is a choice that someone's heart is covered. They make these choices every day. Through kindness and love, though, sometimes they begin to make other choices. That is My hope. So be kind and show them love and mercy.

I know this is difficult to do when someone is mean to you, but know that the meanness is usually not directed at you. It comes from the hard shell covering the heart. Kindness and love often meet the hard shell and deflect the bitterness and anger. Hopefully, love and kindness will eventually break through the shell so that My light can shine through. Remember that it is easy to love the person who is kind, but it is tough to love the difficult ones. That is a true testament to letting them see Me in you.

> *A cheerful heart is good medicine,*
> *but a crushed spirit dries up the bones.*
> (Proverbs 17:22 NIV)

How can you use your heart to be good medicine to those who are difficult to love? How might that be the antidote to help them find God?

Day 226

It is very painful when the heart is broken. Humans have a large capacity to love and to fill the heart. It is painful when someone breaks it. It leaves a scar on the heart, but the heart becomes stronger because of it.

> *Be strong and take heart,*
> *all you who hope in the LORD.*
> (Psalm 31:24 NIV)

How has your trust in God helped you heal a broken heart?

Day 227

Remember that the heart path is always better, but it is often seen as weakness by others. Which is the stronger and more difficult position to take? The heart path. The ego path is what is taught in society. Who is to say it is the correct path? Do not let others influence you as to which path is correct. It is often difficult to be on the heart path. Does this make you weak? Are you considered stronger when you are on the ego path? You are actually stronger and firmer on the heart path.

> *I seek you with all my heart;*
> *do not let me stray from your commands.*
> (Psalm 119:10 NIV)

When has it been easier for you to stray from God's commands than to stray from society's expectations?

Day 228

Your heart is made of Me. You started out as pure love. Then society impacted you, individuals impacted you, and you were molded and shaped. But in the end, your heart will be pure love again. All of the imperfections and scars will be gone when you die; only the pure love will survive. Scars are a result of society. The beauty of the human body is that it heals, but a scar is a reminder of what happened. This makes you "*you*." I heal the heart, and your body heals your body, but you will always have scars. They are not a bad thing but are a reminder of life and what makes you who you are. Once in a while you are reminded of a painful situation, and it hurts. That memory and hurt can be a good thing, for it reminds you of a difficult situation that you overcame with Me. So scars are not necessarily a bad thing. They tell stories of your life. When you die, the scars die as well. You will be in My glory—all love, all the time.

> *I will give you a new heart and put a new spirit in you; I will remove from you your heart of stone and give you a heart of flesh.* (Ezekiel 36:26 NIV)

Do you see your scars as reminders of God's healing?

Day 229

You have a beautiful heart—a heart that I have shaped and molded like a piece of clay. It continues to change and become more beautiful. It is not just good, but it is beautiful. It is beautiful in My eyes. Your heart has gone and will go through heartache, but I have continued to mold it back together again. Are there cracks? Yes, but cracks in porcelain are beautiful, adding beauty to the piece. A totally smooth piece of porcelain is beautiful but lacks character and interest. A cracked heart is more beautiful. Your heart is so beautiful, one of a kind. Continue to let Me mold and shape your heart but never completely buff out the cracks. That is part of the beauty. There are small cracks and there are larger, longer cracks, but all the cracks add to the beauty. No one has a crack-free heart. That is where the phrase "my heart is breaking" comes from. I will seal the broken heart and glue it back together. I am the potter, and you are the clay.

> *But now, O Lord, you are our Father;*
> *we are the clay, and you are our potter;*
> *we are all the work of your hand.*
> (Isaiah 64:8 ESV)

Do you allow God to seal and glue your heart back together?

Day 230

The mind is marvelous. I created it to help man survive. However, the mind has taken over the heart. That was not the intention. Man has decided to live by the mind rather than by the heart. You are happiest when you are living by the heart. Some days you live by the mind, continually thinking about all you need to get done. Write this all down, and then your mind will be satisfied. It has done its job. This will open up the ability to live within your heart. The heart is very powerful. It is where I reside. When you clear the mind, you open up the heart. The heart is where true love is. Get back to living in your heart. Toss that mind clutter away. It is very easy for the mind clutter to take over just a little bit more every day. It is so subtle, but it will happen. Get rid of the worry of the lists of things to do, and get back to your heart. Let your heart go; open it up.

> *Blessed are those who keep his statutes*
> *and seek him with all their heart.*
> (Psalm 119:2 NIV)

What is the difference between seeking God with all your mind and seeking God with all your heart? Which do you do more often?

CHAPTER 18

Control

All you really have control over is yourself and the choices that you make.

Everyone likes to have control over their lives. Some people believe that they can control other people's lives, but this is not true. Ultimately, as we learned earlier, everyone has freedom of choice—the freedom to make their own decisions. Still, many believe they are able to control another person—and perhaps they can for a period of time. But all humans will eventually rebel from being controlled. Even beyond that, God is the one who is really in control. Since God is ultimately in control, isn't it easier just to surrender your life to God and allow Him to guide you in your choices?

Day 231

Control. Everyone likes to be in control, some people more openly than others. However, no one likes to be controlled. As a child, you were controlled by a parent or others. Much of this was for your safety, but so much of it was for conforming to society. Then you began to rebel, usually around two years old, and then again in your teenage years. As a young adult, you craved to be on your own and make your own decisions. That is when you left home; this is part of life. No one wants to be controlled. Every human being will get tired of being controlled, so learn to only control yourself.

> *When I was a child, I talked like a child, I thought like a child, I reasoned like a child. When I became a man, I put the ways of childhood behind me.* (1 Corinthians 13:11 NIV)

Do you like to be controlled? Do you like to control other people? Why?

Day 232

All you really have control over is yourself and the choices that you make. You might think you have control over certain things, like your household. People have to make a choice about whether or not to obey your rules, but ultimately you don't have any control over them if they choose not to obey your rules. It is the person's choice to follow or not follow the rules. You can't do anything about it because you cannot really control them.

> *I appeal to you, brothers, to watch out for those who cause divisions and create obstacles contrary to the doctrine that you have been taught; avoid them. For such persons do not serve our Lord Christ, but their own appetites, and by smooth talk and flattery they deceive the hearts of the naive.* (Romans 16:17–18 ESV)

Do you understand that you only have control over your own actions? Do you try to take control over other people's actions? Do you get upset when you cannot control them?

Day 233

Do you like to be in control? Is this part of who you are? You are learning that you cannot be in control because, ultimately, I am the only one in control. Surrender all to Me. When you get stressed, you tend to tighten your will to try to control everything around you, and then you are not surrendering to Me. Do you see this? Your control is an illusion. You have zero control, yet you still try to control a situation. Do you see how ridiculous that is because I am the one in control? So let it go. I am in control. Why carry this burden? Release it all to Me. Release the illusion of control to Me.

> *For my thoughts are not your thoughts,*
> *neither are your ways my ways,*
> *declares the Lord.*
> *For as the heavens are higher than the earth,*
> *so are my ways higher than your ways*
> *and my thoughts than your thoughts.*
> (Isaiah 55:8–9 ESV)

Do you realize that control is just an illusion and that God is ultimately in control?

CHAPTER 19

The Ego

The ego dies with the body,
but the heart is part of the soul.

The ego versus the heart. Our ego is the part of us that is all of the negatives of society: greed, hate, violence, jealousy, self-righteousness, etc. Our heart is everything that is good and is of God: love, compassion, joy, peace, serenity, etc. When we were born, we were all heart. We did not know the negatives of life. We were so pure and innocent. Then society began to teach us all of the negatives. This is called the ego. In life, there is a constant struggle between the ego and the heart. There are many times we make decisions from the ego and not from the heart. It is important for us to learn the difference. God wants us to be of the heart, of love, of Him. But God also understands how difficult this is for us. He is continually pulling us from ego and into heart. As we learn more about the ego, we are able to do a better job of staying out of the ego and remaining in the heart. We also learn to recognize that many other people are in their ego, and we see the damage caused by it. God wants us to diffuse the ego, whether it is our own ego or that of another. God just wants us to be love.

Day 234

The ego is so powerful. It can take over your life and become your personality. This is not how I intended it to be. I intended you to live from the heart. Still, many people live from the ego and it is a difficult journey. The ego has become very strong. Society reinforces the ego and does not reinforce the heart. Think of the innocence and pureness of a child. People love the innocence and peacefulness of a child. Why? A child loves from the heart. However, society continues to reinforce the ego, so soon a child is not in the heart anymore. The more reinforcement that a child receives for ego-living, the more the child goes into the ego. Society does not reward living from the heart. Society considers that to be weak. It is crazy how being loving, caring, and peaceful is not rewarded, but being arrogant, strong-willed, and non-giving is rewarded. Society needs a shift back to the heart. Everyone struggles with this. Having a close relationship with Me helps you to stay in the heart. Be in the heart, not in the ego.

> *I will remain in the world no longer, but they are still in the world, and I am coming to you. Holy Father, protect them by the power of your name, the name you gave me, so that they may be one as we are one.* (John 17:11 NIV)

In a world and society that encourage pride and boastfulness, how can you live from the heart?

Day 235

Learn to be in your heart and not in your ego. Others will see this and will see the peace that it brings, and they, too, will want to live in their hearts and release their egos. People who are in the ego get a sense of self-worth. When life has beaten them down, they go to the ego. I wish they understood that being in the heart would make them so much happier and would bring them peace. There are many people who live in the ego continuously. This saddens Me, but it is very true. By being in the ego, they are not at peace. They believe that their ego is protecting their heart, but in reality, the ego is causing much more pain. It creates havoc in their life, it creates strife in their life, and it creates unrest in their life. The ego lashes out at people—at parents, children, friends, and others with whom they come in contact. This causes even more unhappiness. If they could learn to be in their heart more, they would have so much peace in their life. So practice being in your heart. Smash your ego down. Do not let it rear its ugly head.

> *For where you have envy and selfish ambition, there you find disorder and every evil practice.* (James 3:16 NIV)

Have you seen the disorder caused by envy and selfish ambition? How can you squash the ego and live from the heart?

Day 236

The ego dies with the body, but the heart is part of the soul. The best of someone, the true self, the soul, is what will go to heaven, not the ego. So which do you want to cultivate on Earth—the heart or the ego? It is a very simple question, and yet cultivating the heart can be very difficult to do, especially with all of the pressures of society. It is so easy to push the heart away. However, I give you the strength to push the ego aside and bring out the heart. The more you push down the ego, the easier it becomes to live from the heart and to be your true self. When the ego is dominant, you will feel uncomfortable. That is a sign that you are pushing your heart away and pushing Me away. Call to Me, and I will help you to squash the ego. This takes much practice because you were conditioned to be in the ego from a very young age.

> *People give birth to people. But the Spirit gives birth to spirit.* (John 3:6)

Have you ever really considered that the ego dies with the body and the heart is part of the soul? Which are you choosing to cultivate?

Day 237

A foggy day when the blue sky begins breaking through is similar to the ego cracking and the light of the heart beginning to shine. Look up and see the clouds and fog, and watch as more and more of the blue sky appears. The heart and soul are the beautiful blue sky, and the ego is the dark and grey clouds. Continue to watch as the sky becomes more and more prominent and the clouds/ego begin to dissipate and disappear. Soon the fog and clouds will be gone. There will be no evidence of them. There will be a bright, sunny blue sky. Occasionally, storms and fog will come and cover the light, but call to Me, and soon the sun will come out again.

> *He stilled the storm to a whisper;*
> *the waves of the sea were hushed.*
> (Psalm 107:29 NIV)

Are you living your days in the fog (ego) or in the sunshine (heart)? Do you allow God to be the light in your life to break down the fog/ego?

Day 238

Live in your heart, not in your mind/ego. Keep the ego at bay. When you feel the ego coming out, let it go. Call to Me, and I will come to you from your heart. Join Me in your heart. There are many evils in the world, such as the love of money, greed, sex, drugs, selfishness, and so many other things that pull you from Me. These things all bring temporary pleasures and immediate gratification. It is easy to move to the ego to satisfy self. Now that you know how to live in your heart with Me, you will feel uncomfortable when you live in your ego. You will begin to recognize it. When you are in the ego or are moving into the ego, you will feel it. Call to Me to help you return to your heart.

> *Therefore tell the people: This is what the* L*ORD* *Almighty says: "Return to me," declares the* L*ORD* *Almighty, "and I will return to you," says the* L*ORD* *Almighty.* (Zechariah 1:3 NIV)

Has living in your ego ever come between you and your relationship with God?

Day 239

Let's go deeper into the ego. This is a very important part of My teaching, and for some people, it is the most difficult. Becoming aware of when the ego is present is actually the easiest part. Diffusing the ego before it causes harm is probably the most difficult part. Many people are in the ego most of the time. That is not how I intended it to be, but society has brought out the ego. Get rid of these negative feelings, and be in the heart with love, peace, generosity, and kindness. Whenever you feel negativity, you are in the ego. Call to Me, and go to the heart. Emotions of hurt will bring out the ego quickly on both sides. The ego becomes a false protector—a shield—of feelings. Instead, put on a shield of love and go to the heart.

> *For if you live according to the flesh, you will die; but if by the Spirit you put to death the misdeeds of the body, you will live.* (Romans 8:13 NIV)

Why is the ego one of God's most difficult teachings? Can you become more and more a person of the heart each day?

Day 240

When the heart is so covered up, it is hard to feel the pull toward Me. You have had many things pull you away. Then I finally tugged so hard that you came to Me with open arms. Yet the tug toward the ego is still there pulling you. It is a tug-of-war game with the ego on one side and the heart/Me on the other. Just when you are about to go over the line to the heart, there is something in the ego that pulls you back—something such as greed, lust, anger, material things, drugs, alcohol, or the things of society. It tugs at you—but let Me pull harder to keep you from falling over the line. The closer you get to Me, the stronger the ego will try to pull you back. But know that I am your God and I will continue to pull you toward Me. Open your eyes, feel My strength, and let Me pull you over the line to Me.

> *For you were called to freedom, brothers. Only do not use your freedom as an opportunity for the flesh, but through love serve one another. For the whole law is fulfilled in one word: "You shall love your neighbor as yourself." But if you bite and devour one another, watch out that you are not consumed by one another.*
> (Galatians 5:13–15 ESV)

What is winning the battle in your life right now—the heart or the ego?

Day 241

Awareness is the key. First, you learn about the ego, and then you learn to realize when you are in ego. Finally, you learn how to get out of ego. What can be even more difficult, though, is not going to ego in the first place. This is done by living in your heart and being in My presence.

> *Those who are in the flesh cannot please God.*
> (Romans 8:8 ESV)

What measures are you taking each day to be in your heart instead of in your ego?

Day 242

It is very easy for the ego to take over, to live by the ego and not by the heart. Be in your heart, not in your ego. How do you recognize that you are in ego? It will be uncomfortable. You will not feel like yourself. You will not be living in love. When you start to concern yourself and judge other people's actions, you are living in ego. It feels uncomfortable. Call to Me, and I will bring you back to the heart. As time goes on, it will become easier and easier to recognize when you are in ego. Release yourself back to Me, to your heart.

> *There is only one Lawgiver and Judge. He is the God who is able to save life or destroy it. But who are you to judge your neighbor?* (James 4:12)

Judgmentalism is one indicator that you are in ego. What are some other common warning signs that you are not living out of your heart, that you are not living out of love?

Day 243

Anger is another component to being in ego. When you feel this emotion, you are probably already there. When you are angry, step back and ask yourself if this is because you are in ego. Also, be aware of those around you. They will pull you into ego very easily. Learn to walk away. Learn not to discuss it. Learn to ask Me for help. I will always tell you if you are in ego, and I will help return you to your heart.

> *Human anger doesn't produce the holy life God wants.* (James 1:20)

Think about the last time you were angry. Were you living in ego or from your heart (love)?

Day 244

I know that you get angry at times and go to ego. You know that you are in ego but you can't seem to pull yourself out. Sometimes this takes incredible strength. You may be pressured by others to be angry. Take a step back and wait before reacting. Then you will be able to respond from your heart with love instead of in anger from the ego.

> *Do not let the sun go down while you are still angry.* (Ephesians 4:26)

Has your ego caused you to let the sun go down while you were still angry? Did it become easier or harder to let go of that anger the longer you waited?

Day 245

Being lazy and selfish are qualities of the ego. Once the ego has a strong foothold on someone, those nasty qualities are there. Know that this is not one's heart. Try to remember this when you react and go to your ego. Remember, too, that many people do not even know they are in ego.

> *A person's wisdom makes them patient.*
> *They will be honored if they forgive someone*
> *who sins against them.* (Proverbs 19:11)

Do you see the wisdom in learning about the ego? How is it easier to forgive someone when you understand they are coming from a place of ego?

Day 246

The ego will pull you away from Me. It is so easily done. There are so many pressures from society, so many things to do. Become aware of the ego. When the ego comes out, call to Me. It is very easy for the ego to rear its ugly head. You can tell when the ego is around because you become uncomfortable. You will feel this discomfort, whether it is from anger, jealousy, rage, selfishness, or any other negative attribute. When you are feeling any of these emotions, you are more than likely in ego. Call to Me and release the ego. I will help you to do this.

> *Then you will call, and the Lord will answer;*
> *you will cry for help, and he will say: Here am I.*
> *"If you do away with the yoke of oppression,*
> *with the pointing finger and malicious talk, . . .*
> *then your light will rise in the darkness,*
> *and your night will become like the noonday."*
> (Isaiah 58:9–10 NIV)

How often do you find yourself in ego? Are you able to pull yourself out of ego and into your heart?

Day 247

Life does not need to be so difficult. Humans make it difficult. Just looking at everything from a different perspective can really change things. Learn how feelings quickly bring out the ego. Learn how someone else's feelings bring out your ego. Really work to stay out of the ego. It is difficult, but realizing you are in ego is an important step. Look at every situation when you are experiencing negative feelings; take a step back and turn it into a loving situation. If you can do this, you will be able to pull yourself out of the ego. It is simple in concept yet very difficult to do. Practice doing this daily. It is not just recognizing that you are in ego, but it also involves pulling yourself out of ego, and then reacting in a loving way.

> *What causes fights and quarrels among you? Don't they come from your desires that battle within you?* (James 4:1 NIV)

The battle within you is the constant battle between the heart and the ego. Do you see how your ego causes many fights among those you love?

Day 248

That uncomfortable feeling that you feel inside is your ego. Handle your disagreements with love and kindness. Speak to someone about a situation in a loving and kind way, and stay out of ego. Just talking about the situation will often release it and satisfy the ego. If you do not speak in a kind and loving way, the other person's ego will flare, and in turn, yours will flare too. When you don't talk about a situation, it will often fester. It continues to build. Then your ego will make a mountain out of a molehill. You begin to concentrate on it. Whatever the ego concentrates on expands. Soon it will get too big, and the ego will release it. You become very angry, and what you say does not come out in a kind and loving way. Learn to talk about a situation first rather than exploding in a non-loving way after you let it fester. It is never a good thing when the ego takes the lead.

> *If your brother sins against you, go and tell him his fault, between you and him alone. If he listens to you, you have gained your brother.*
> (Matthew 18:15 ESV)

Can you think of a time when you have allowed a situation to fester too long? What might have been different about the outcome if you had gone directly to the other person in a kind and loving way right away?

Day 249

When someone is annoying you, look at the reasons. Why are you upset, and where does this come from? It comes from your ego. Do you want your ego to be a ruler in your life? Is this comfortable? No, it is uncomfortable. Your gut bothers you, and your heart beats faster. Just release the situation to Me and let it go. Focus on the important things in life—your loved ones and Me. If it does not affect these, then let it go. Do not waste time and space on things that do not matter on your journey. Let them go. All they do is take up space from Me.

> *Let all bitterness and wrath and anger and clamor and slander be put away from you, along with all malice.* (Ephesians 4:31 ESV)

How can you release situations that really do not affect your life?

Day 250

Many poor choices that are made are made from the ego. The ego is making too many decisions. You need to make your decisions from your heart. The saying *What would Jesus do?* (WWJD) is so wise. If you are making a decision based on the ego, then it is wrong. If it is based on the heart—WWJD?—then it is right.

> *For to this you have been called, because Christ also suffered for you, leaving you an example, so that you might follow in his steps.*
> (1 Peter 2:21 ESV)

What decisions are you facing right now? What would Jesus do? What would He choose if He had your same options?

Day 251

Many people are in deep ego all the time. The events of society have led them there. They have been so hurt or so taken by the evil of society that they cannot make their way back to the heart. You can tell this because deep down, they are not happy.

> *So also you have sorrow now, but I will see you again, and your hearts will rejoice, and no one will take your joy from you.* (John 16:22 ESV)

Do you know someone who appears to live their life in ego? How do you prevent them from taking your joy?

Day 252

It is okay to have feelings. I gave them to you. You can't help how you feel. Do your best to take a step back and look at a situation. Is it really worth getting upset about and moving into ego? Instead, be happy about those who are around you. Be happy for the friends you have. Be happy for Me in your life. Be happy for your children. Be happy for your spouse. Do not let those who hurt your feelings send you into ego. Instead, flip it around so that you are able to rejoice in those who are in your life. Feelings are in the heart, but the mind will blow them out of proportion. When your feelings are hurt, consider why, but do not let it go to the ego. Just say to yourself, *Hey, my feelings are hurt*, and move on.

> *My dear friends, don't try to get even. Leave room for God to show his anger.* (Romans 12:19)

Is there a person or a situation when your feelings were hurt and you went to ego and confronted someone? What was the result?

Day 253

Everyone has an ego, and it can be really hard to control—especially when your feelings have been hurt. If you speak to someone who has hurt your feelings, come from your heart. Remember, though, that even when you do this, the other person may feel as if he needs to justify having hurt you. He wants to justify his actions so you understand that it was not intentional. But your ego does not like this answer, and the ego wants to make sure that he knows he hurt you no matter what his intention was. It often then becomes ego versus ego, and the result is a fight. To diffuse this situation, acknowledge his viewpoint—that he meant no harm and did not mean to hurt you—and give forgiveness.

> *But to you who are listening I say: Love your enemies, do good to those who hate you, bless those who curse you, pray for those who mistreat you.* (Luke 6:27–28 NIV)

Do you understand that most people do not want to intentionally hurt you?

Day 254

Just like in a cartoon when there is an angel on one shoulder and the devil on the other, so it is with the ego and the heart. The devil is always trying to persuade you to do what is bad, and the angel is trying to convince you to do what is good. In the cartoon, you can see the pressure the person is under by the ego (devil), but you can also see the pressure the person is under by the heart (angel); typically, after a struggle, the angel prevails.

> *He replied, "Instead, blessed are those who hear God's word and obey it."* (Luke 11:28)

Do you often feel as if you have an angel and a devil on your shoulders? Do you feel the struggle? Does your angel usually win, or does your devil usually win?

CHAPTER 20

Boundaries

It is okay to put up a boundary between you and another person.

It is okay to put up a boundary between you and another person, especially between you and someone who is continually hurting you and causing you strife. This gives you an opportunity to distance yourself from the person and to see the person and the situation more clearly. With this space, God urges us to pray for that person and to find forgiveness through prayer. Your boundaries might be different than other people's boundaries. It is important to respect the boundaries of others, just as they need to respect yours.

Day 255

It is okay to put up a boundary between you and another person. This enables you to step away from the pain they cause, create some space, and pray for them. I understand that it is very difficult to do this, but once you have space, you will be able to pray for that person. Then something beautiful happens: forgiveness. You are able to forgive. You are able to see things more clearly because with praying comes compassion and forgiveness. It is truly beautiful. It is okay to put up and keep your boundary. Observe the pain the person is in; then pray and forgive.

> *Let your foot be seldom in your neighbor's house,*
> *lest he have his fill of you and hate you.*
> (Proverbs 25:17 ESV)

Do you see how a boundary gives you distance and space to pray for and forgive someone?

Day 256

It is okay to put up a boundary and stick with it. Will the boundary shift over time? More than likely it will, but it is your boundary to put up and move. It is no one else's. You are doing this for your well-being. You know your limits, and others need to respect them. Others may have different boundaries than you do. You should not ask others to move their boundaries, and they should not ask you to move yours. Other people need to move their boundaries on their own for their own well-being, and you are not respecting them if you ask them to move them.

> *Finally, brothers, rejoice. Aim for restoration, comfort one another, agree with one another, live in peace; and the God of love and peace will be with you.* (2 Corinthians 13:11 ESV)

What boundaries have you put up, or what boundaries do you need to put up, to bring you peace?

CHAPTER 21

Do not let your stresses weaken your spirit.
Be strong. Let Me heal you.
Let Me be your light.

Do you allow stress to take over your life? Have you often wondered why you are sick a lot of the time? Do you realize the correlation between stress and illness? God teaches us that stress wreaks havoc on our bodies. There is only so much stress that the human body can take. God wants us to let Him carry our burdens and take our stress away. He understands how difficult this is for us. He wants us to call to Him and ask Him for guidance and help.

Day 257

There might be times when you have a busy few days with a lot of worry and stress. That is totally normal. Take a deep breath and calm down. Be with Me and come back to peace. When life is stressful, it can be tough to get back to peace. The goal is to stay at peace in the first place. I understand that this is difficult. It is difficult for everyone, so take a few steps back and be with Me. When you feel stressed, call to Me.

> *Worry makes the heart heavy.*
> *But a kind word cheers it up.* (Proverbs 12:25)

When you are stressed and worried, can you take a few steps back and call to God for help? What happens?

Day 258

Slow down with your worries and stress. They will eventually fill you up and need to be released. Through surrender, all the stress will begin to seep out of your body. It may have taken a long time to get into this position, so it will take a long time to get out of this position. Stress can be a difficult thing to deal with. Don't take it on alone, but surrender it to Me. Look back on your life and see that I have taken care of all of your problems. Just turn them over to Me.

> *Therefore I tell you, do not worry about your life, what you will eat or drink; or about your body, what you will wear. Is not life more than food, and the body more than clothes?*
> (Matthew 6:25 NIV)

Do you allow your worries and stress to take over your life? What can you surrender to God?

Day 259

Do not worry and create stress. Stress weakens the body—not only on the inside, but also on the outside. You need to release all of your stress to Me or your body will become weak. Do not let your stress weaken your spirit. Be strong. Let Me heal you. Let Me be your light. Stress affects not only your heart but also your body. Strengthen both with Me.

> *Do you not know that your body is a temple of the Holy Spirit within you, whom you have from God? You are not your own, for you were bought with a price. So glorify God in your body.*
> (1 Corinthians 6:19–20 ESV)

How are you allowing stress to harm your body? What is a cause of stress that you can surrender today to God?

Day 260

Surrender stress. When you feel nervousness in your stomach, let it go. Surrender. Breathe in the Holy Spirit to help you. Feel the calmness wash over you. Feel My love. Feel My arms embrace you. Come to Me in union. You and Me. How joyful! How beautiful! So joyful, so beautiful, and without a care in the world—like a dog playing with a toy. Live like this. Remember the joy that you feel with Me. Show joy and peace.

> *And he said to his disciples, "Therefore I tell you, do not be anxious about your life, what you will eat, nor about your body, what you will put on."*
> (Luke 12:22 ESV)

Think of something that you are anxious about right now. Pray and breathe in the Holy Spirit to help you. What happened?

Day 261

Stress is an ugly thing. It is blackness and darkness within your body. It must come out and be relieved or it will cause havoc within. Stress can come out as illness, anger, tension, headaches, and many other things. Let go of the stress, release the darkness, and your aches and pains will heal. This is yet another reason to surrender.

> *Cast your burden on the* L*ORD*,
> *and he will sustain you;*
> *he will never permit*
> *the righteous to be moved.*
> (Psalm 55:22 ESV)

How does stress come out in you? Does it come out in illness? In anger? Does your body become weak with stress? Why do you not surrender your burdens to God?

Day 262

In everything, even in times of stress, there is an opportunity to grow in faith. Your aches and pains caused by stress will heal. Just have patience and surrender to Me. Release it all to Me.

> *Out of my distress I called on the LORD;*
> *the LORD answered me and set me free.*
> *The LORD is on my side; I will not fear.*
> *What can man do to me?*
> (Psalm 118:5–6 ESV)

Have you ever tried to really release stress by surrendering to God? Were you set free from your aches and pains?

Day 263

Stress wreaks havoc on the body. When you are stressed, the body becomes tight and injury occurs. If this is what stress is doing to the outside of your body, imagine what stress does to the inside of your body! So here is the lesson. Surrender all aspects of your life and relax. You will heal on both the inside and the outside. Once you do this, you will feel better. From here on out, enjoy all aspects of your beautiful life—and relax.

> *It is in vain that you rise up early*
> *and go late to rest,*
> *eating the bread of anxious toil;*
> *for he gives to his beloved sleep.*
> (Psalm 127:2 ESV)

How much longer before you surrender your stress to God and relax?

Day 264

Your body will always teach you what your mind will not allow. Your mind is telling you to be perfect in many aspects, but your body is telling you that it is not able to handle the stress of trying to be perfect. Be happy where you are in all aspects of your life. Just be happy. It is okay to strive to be better, but there is no need for perfection. Do you understand?

> *For all have sinned and fall short*
> *of the glory of God.* (Romans 3:23 ESV)

Do you understand the difference between striving to be better and being perfect?

Day 265

One of the beauties of illness is that it is truly awesome when you feel better. You know what it is like to feel terrible and have your body not well, and then when you are well, you appreciate feeling good. It is the same when you are in heart, your true self; you feel so good, but when the ego takes over, you don't feel good. You learn how good it feels to be in the true self/heart as opposed to being in the ego. This is how you will always want to be.

> *Because of how I suffered for Christ, I'm glad that I am weak. I am glad in hard times. I am glad when people say mean things about me. I am glad when things are difficult. And I am glad when people make me suffer. When I am weak, I am strong.* (2 Corinthians 12:10)

Do you ever appreciate how great it is to feel good after an illness? Have you ever equated this to the feeling of being one with God as opposed to when you are not one with Him?

Day 266

Your stress may be high right now. What causes stress? Stress is caused by not surrendering all to Me. Think about it. If you surrender all to Me and trust in Me, what is there to stress about?

> *So commit yourself to God completely.*
> *Reach out your hands to him for help.*
> (Job 11:13)

Since you know that stress is the lack of surrender, what are you waiting for?

CHAPTER 22

Strife, Struggles, and Storms

I will guide you through the storm. I am the lighthouse, the bright light in the storm. Just continue to keep your eyes on the light.

Strife, struggles, and storms will always happen in your life. God wants us to see the beauty in them. He tells us that these are facts of life, but He also tells us that if we fortify our houses with Him, we will be able to weather the storms. He wants us to go through the storms with Him, because with Him, the severity of the storms will lessen. There are also many lessons to learn from these storms. God asks us to look at the storms and see the lessons as well as the blessings.

Day 267

The battle is over, and it appears that evil is the victor. But the war is not over. Sometimes battles have to be lost in order for the war to be won. It may appear that evil is winning, but you have Me, God, on your side. Evil will not win out. It never does. Trust Me on this. This battle needed to be lost. I needed to get you out of this situation and keep you free from harm. It may not be evident now, but it will be evident when you look back on all of this. This battle was lost in order to protect you in the battles to come. There is a strategy that sometimes it is best to lose or concede a battle in order to win the war. Sometimes it is best for the troops to withdraw. Sometimes it is best to let the enemy believe they have won the war. In reality, it was just a small battle. So take a rest; this battle is over. I have removed you from the war. I will fight the rest of the war. I will take care of all of this.

> *He gives me new strength.*
> *He guides me in the right paths*
> *for the honor of his name.* (Psalm 23:3)

Has it ever seemed to you that evil had won and you had lost a battle only to realize later that it was just God removing you from the war?

Day 268

As you know, everyone has strife. It can either destroy you or make you stronger. It can either fortify your house or weaken it.

> *My brothers and sisters, you will face all kinds of trouble. When you do, think of it as pure joy. Your faith will be tested. You know that when this happens it will produce in you the strength to continue.* (James 1:2–3)

Do you let strife destroy you, or do you let strife make you stronger? What does it mean when God says to fortify your house? How do you do this?

Day 269

There are so many positives in life, but I know that the negatives can overpower you—and that can be difficult. Life has its struggles—sometimes big and sometimes small—but they are all struggles. It is easy to throw yourself a little pity party. Things are not how you wanted or believed them to be. Nothing is that way. To get absorbed in this will lead to non-peace and anxiety—both things you don't wish for. I know this can be disappointing for you, but when you focus on the negative, it will always expand. When you focus on the positive, it will also expand. So when you are feeling down, breathe Me in. This is an opportunity to feel My presence, and it is also a reminder that I am right here with you.

> *You were taught to be made new in your thinking.*
> (Ephesians 4:23)

Do you tend to focus on the negative or on the positive?

Day 270

The calm before the storm—this is the way of life. Life is a series of calmness and storms. Some are just rain showers, others are thunderstorms, and still others are hurricanes. How much protection do you have from the storm? Are you protected by a grass hut or a concrete house? With Me at your side, you have a concrete house. But if the house is not on a solid foundation, it will not weather the storms. Build your house on a solid foundation made of concrete. You will always weather the storm.

> *So then, everyone who hears my words and puts them into practice is like a wise man. He builds his house on the rock.* (Matthew 7:24)

Have you built your house on the rock of trusting God? How can you fortify your house for life's inevitable storms?

Day 271

I will guide you through the storm. I am the lighthouse, the bright light in the storm. Just continue to keep your eyes on the light.

> *Again Jesus spoke to them, saying, "I am the light of the world. Whoever follows me will not walk in darkness, but will have the light of life."*
> (John 8:12 ESV)

Think of a past storm. Was God your lighthouse, or did you try to weather the storm in darkness on your own?

Day 272

There are many times when you wonder why you have so many storms. These storms help you grow with Me. They help you to become the person I want you to be. Look back at so many lessons. Could you have learned these lessons without strife? Of course not. Your lessons and experiences are for our journey—to help you and Me become one, to help you obtain a relationship with Me. It may not seem like such a beautiful gift during the storms, but you can later see that the results of the storms—flowers, birds, trees, fruit—are all beautiful. They would not be there, though, without the storms. The true gift of Me is the result and outcome of the storms—faith, trust, and love of life—our relationship. Let's continue to flourish. The mustard seed will continue to grow into a large shrub that will house many birds and so much fruit. This is My gift to you.

> *And Jesus answered them, "Have faith in God. Truly, I say to you, whoever says to this mountain, 'Be taken up and thrown into the sea,' and does not doubt in his heart, but believes that what he says will come to pass, it will be done for him. Therefore I tell you, whatever you ask in prayer, believe that you have received it, and it will be yours."* (Mark 11:22–24 ESV)

Do you now understand that a storm brings you gifts?

Day 273

I will protect you in times of storms, but always remember that there is a lesson to be taught by the storm. Storms can become a gift of faith to you. Do not dread the storms, but instead look at them in wonder. Be amazed in anticipation of how I will fix things and work it all out. Then your faith becomes stronger and stronger—strengthening your house. Also enjoy the sunshine, with the peace of the light of the sun shining in the window and the warmth upon your skin. It is truly beautiful and peaceful. I know sometimes it feels as if you have had more storms than sunshine, but this has fortified your house. Enjoy the sunshine upon your face, but will there be more storms? Of course, but your house is stronger and these storms will be less severe with Me!

> *And everything I've taught you is so that the peace which is in me will be in you and will give you great confidence as you rest in me. For in this unbelieving world you will experience trouble and sorrows, but you must be courageous, for I have conquered the world!* (John 16:33 TPT)

During your next storm, ask yourself in wonder how God will work this out.

Day 274

Sometimes you think that it is summer, and then you have an unexpected snowstorm. But goodness comes out of the storm. The reservoirs are fuller, the water nourishes the grass, and the trees are pruned; so much beauty comes from the storm. You can also wallow in the storm. It is cold, the trees are breaking, the flowers are dying, and you have to shovel. You have no control over when storms happen and how severe they are. You knew yesterday that it was coming, so you prepared. You covered your flowers and drained your sprinkler. Yes, you prepared, but you had no idea how severe the storm would be. It is the same with your life. You have no control over the timing or severity of the storm, but you can prepare. Build your house strong, and continue to fortify your house. Be prepared with Me, and you will weather the storms.

> *I would hurry to my place of safety.*
> *It would be far away from the winds and*
> *storms I'm facing.* (Psalm 55:8)

Are you able to see what a blessing it is to have a constant refuge from storms through your relationship with God?

Day 275

All things calm down after a while. You must weather the storm, and you will experience the calm after the storm. You know more storms will come. This is life as it is in nature. There is calmness, and there are storms. The storms are of varying degrees and duration. Life mirrors nature in this way.

> *Suffering city, you have been beaten by storms.*
> *You have not been comforted.*
> *I will rebuild you with turquoise stones.*
> *I will rebuild your foundations with lapis lazuli.* (Isaiah 54:11)

When you look at your life, do you see it as a series of storms and calmness? Do you understand that this is life?

Day 276

There are always storms on the horizon, but if you have fortified your house, you can handle all of them—even the most severe. Make your foundation strong and your roof strong, and your house will not falter during the storm. Storms are always coming. This is part of nature, for with the storms come the rain and then the sunshine so that life can grow. In the spring, look around you and see all the green, the birds in trees, and the beautiful flowers and plants. What brings the spring? The winter storms, of course. Know that no matter what storms come, your house is strong and the storms lead to much beauty. When a blizzard comes, you will be snug in your home, warm and safe.

> *Then I will remember my covenant between me and you and every kind of living creature. The waters will never again become a flood to destroy all life.* (Genesis 9:15)

Do you see the calmness in your life after a storm?

CHAPTER 23

Relationships and Marriage

All relationships need to be cultivated and fertilized in order to grow.

God teaches us that relationships take time. You need to take the time to be with your spouse, children, and friends. If you do not, you will begin to feel disconnected, and the relationships will fail. This is especially true with God. You need to continually cultivate your relationship with Him by spending time with Him and continually having space with Him. If you do not do this, you will find that your relationship with God will begin to falter. It is not that God is not there, but it is that you are not there with Him. So continue to cultivate all of your relationships!

Marriage can be difficult. God teaches us to stay out of the ego and to be in our heart with our true self. Many people let the ego get in the way of their marriage. They begin to feel that they are better than the other person, and then they begin to lose respect for their spouse. Your true self tells you that you are both equals and are both doing the best you can. God tells us to stay out of ego and to be in our heart. It is also extremely important to have God in the center of your marriage. When doing this, you can ask God for help and guidance with your marriage.

For those of you who are not married, this is still a beautiful opportunity to learn, for many of these lessons will apply to a possible future spouse, as well as to the many other relationships in your life!

Day 277

I want My children to be able to discuss with each other things that are bothering them. When you have problems, this does not mean that the relationship is bad, but it is an opportunity to grow closer together. Just like when problems happen in life, it is an opportunity to grow closer to Me. Problems have the potential to make relationships stronger, but many people choose to let them weaken a relationship. Use problems to strengthen them.

> *Do to others as you want them to do to you.*
> (Luke 6:31)

Do you use problems in your relationship as an opportunity to grow closer together or to grow further apart? Are you able to discuss an issue with another person with love, just as you want them to discuss an issue with you?

Day 278

A connection with your spouse is important, but a connection with Me is even more important. The connection with Me, though, is fragile. What happens when you don't spend time with Me? There is a disconnect, a disjointed feeling about your day. That is an indication of a failing relationship. It is also difficult to get back, so it is easier to just spend time with Me every day and maintain that connection. Always make time for Me, and also make time for your significant other, children, and friends. Time is very precious. Spend it wisely. You never get it back. Do not let the things of this world get in the way of what is important in your life.

> *These people honor me by what they say.*
> *But their hearts are far away from me.*
> (Matthew 15:8)

Do you understand how fragile your relationship with God is? Do you feel a disconnect when you don't spend time with Him? Have you experienced how difficult it is to get that relationship back?

Day 279

All relationships need to be cultivated and fertilized to grow. Many marriages and relationships fail because they lack these things. People grow apart. They do not spend time together. Their time is spent on other earthly things. Do not lose sight of this. Continue to make time for each other.

> *Husbands, love your wives. Love them just as Christ loved the church. He gave himself up for her.* (Ephesians 5:25)

Have you grown apart from your spouse? Do you spend too much time with your earthly things and love them more than your significant other? How can you make more time for your significant other?

Day 280

I created all of My children the same, and yet very different. What makes these differences? The differences are caused by society, the way you were raised, your parents, and your friends. Every human is different. Figuring out your spouse's needs is very important. It is one of the ways that you show your love for each other. Relationships ebb and flow. They are not still. The way you have shown your love in the past might need to be adjusted. This is due to the experiences that people have. In a relationship, you have to be aware of these changes and continually show your love in the way that your spouse needs—and your spouse needs to be aware of this as well. Relationships are not static but are always changing. Each person needs to adapt to the other person in order to have a successful marriage. Be awake and aware to what your spouse needs. This awakening will help your marriage to succeed. People tend to get lazy in their relationships. Don't let this happen to you.

> *Be loving in everything you do.*
> (1 Corinthians 16:14)

Do you take the time to figure out your spouse's needs and then act upon them?

Day 281

There will be times when you feel distanced from your spouse. This is normal, but when you feel this way, take a step back and make time for each other—reconnect. You may have had a busy week. You might have stress. So make the time to reconnect. Do the same with Me. When you get busy, stop and take time for Me. When you lose space, you lose space for Me, and not only for Me, but also for your spouse. Keep time for those you love. Make it a priority. Remember what is important in your life.

> *For the Spirit God gave us does not make us timid,*
> *but gives us power, love and self-discipline.*
> (2 Timothy 1:7 NIV)

Do you see the damage that your busyness causes in your life, with your significant other, and with God?

Day 282

All throughout your life, there will always be others to whom you are attracted. There may come a point in your life when you make the decision to be with one specific person and get married. The initial attraction will fade, so it is important to marry someone with the same morals and ethics and whose company you enjoy. You make that decision to marry, but sometimes you may have an attraction to someone else. Then a choice needs to be made. Hopefully, that choice is to stay faithful to the one whom you married. Some people give in to this temptation. They give up their love and their marriage for a brief encounter. This is free will. This is adultery. They break My commandments for a brief moment of pleasure.

> *You are tempted in the same way all other human beings are. God is faithful. He will not let you be tempted any more than you can take. But when you are tempted, God will give you a way out. Then you will be able to deal with it.*
> (1 Corinthians 10:13)

Have you ever been attracted to someone other than your spouse? What did you do? Did you turn to God for help?

Day 283

Society today has turned into a "me" society. This pulls people to make incorrect choices. People have also fallen away from Me. This also leads to incorrect decisions. People are looking for Me, but they fill that void with poor relationships. They are not getting what they need from one person, so they move from person to person searching for it. The search is actually the search for Me to fill the void in their lives, not the search for another meaningless relationship.

> *For all that is in the world—the desires of the flesh and the desires of the eyes and pride of life—is not from the Father but is from the world.*
> (1 John 2:15 ESV)

Are you trying to fill a void in your life with the desires of the flesh? Do you now understand that you will always be unsatisfied because this void needs to be filled with God?

Day 284

People need to understand that it takes much time to get to know a future spouse. They also need to understand the seriousness of this commitment. You will learn much from different relationships. You will figure out what traits work with your traits. The initial physical attraction will fade. The next attraction is to make the commitment to truly love the other person. This becomes a new type of attraction—love. Many people do not ever get to this level, but they marry anyway. This causes many relationships to fail. Teach your children the difference between the initial physical attraction and love. They are truly different. Of course, marriage is even more difficult without having Me at the center.

> *Here is my command. Love one another, just as I have loved you.* (John 15:12)

Have you made the choice to truly love another person as God has loved you?

Day 285

Many people look at difficulties as a bad thing, but they are only bad if you do not communicate. If you communicate, you can work things out and strengthen your relationship. If you do not discuss the difficulties, they fester, stories are created, and the difficulties increase. They may even become too great to overcome. So communicate and find out what is wrong. Then things can be fixed, and a deeper love will follow.

> *Let your speech always be gracious, seasoned with salt, so that you may know how you ought to answer each person.* (Colossians 4:6 ESV)

Have you ever experienced a difficulty and then worked it out and found a deeper love?

Day 286

Somehow the sanctity of marriage has gone downhill. The evils of life have gotten in the way. The self-centeredness of people has gotten in the way. Choosing a mate for life is very serious. People are not taking it that way. If marriage gets too difficult, they give up and divorce. Marriage is not always easy, but with Me at the center of your marriage, it will be successful. Know that I need to be the center of both your lives and your marriage. It is not just man and woman together. It is man, woman, and Me.

> *One person could be overpowered.*
> *But two people can stand up for themselves.*
> *And a rope made out of three cords isn't easily broken.* (Ecclesiastes 4:12)

Do you see the importance of having God at the center of your marriage—of having three cords?

Day 287

Many marriages take place every day where I am not at the center. Some marriages make it, and some do not. I am always there, but many people do not acknowledge My presence. When I am acknowledged, problems are much easier to get through. Having faith, knowing I will help you get through the difficult times, makes a huge difference. Turning to Me in the good times as well as in the bad times will help a marriage to last, to be happy, and to be joyful.

> *Follow the lead of one another because of your respect for Christ.* (Ephesians 5:21)

Do you and your spouse turn to God in the bad times? What about in the good times?

Day 288

Put your faith in Me to strengthen your marriage. Put your faith in Me to solve your problems. Put your faith in Me to weather the storms. This will strengthen your marriage. I know that there are tough times in life and in marriage, but together we can weather the storms.

> *Without faith it is impossible to please God, because anyone who comes to him must believe that he exists and that he rewards those who earnestly seek him.* (Hebrews 11:6 NIV)

Do you and your spouse face the storms in your marriage together, separately, or with all three of you (you, your spouse, and God)?

Day 289

Let's talk about respect in the marriage. It is vital that both people respect each other. The ego may get in the way of respect. When one spouse's ego flares and that person begins to feel "better" than the other person, respect begins to fade. When respect fades, the ego gets bigger. As this happens, respect fades even more. Love fades along with the respect, and this is disastrous. Why does this happen? The ego. The ego wants to be better than and superior to the other person. Do not let the ego take over and cause you to want to feel superior.

> *Love is not happy with evil. But it is full of joy when the truth is spoken. It always protects. It always trusts. It always hopes. It never gives up.* (1 Corinthians 13:6–7)

Does your ego get in the way of your relationship? Do you see how this leads to disrespecting your spouse?

Day 290

Just because you would do something differently does not mean the other person's way is wrong. It is just different. Do not let your ego come out and cause you to lose respect for the other person. Who is to say that your spouse's way is not right for them? From your viewpoint, you may not think that it is right for your spouse, but from your spouse's viewpoint, it is. Each of you will be in danger of losing respect for the other person. Do not let this happen. Keep the ego away. Have respect for the way the situation is handled by the other person. Mistakes will be made. Do not let the ego come out and be the "I told you so." That is ego, and it leads to disrespect. Let it go, knowing that your spouse is doing their best.

> *Make my joy complete by being of the same mind, maintaining the same love, united in spirit, intent on one purpose. Do nothing from selfishness or empty conceit, but with humility of mind regard one another as more important than yourselves.* (Philippians 2:2–3 NASB1995)

Do you believe that your way of doing things is always right? Do you see the damage that this can cause in your marriage?

Day 291

Marriage is a balancing act, and you need to find that balance—like a person balancing plates in both hands. What is the balance? When too many plates are stacked on one side, they fall and crash. How many plates need to be in each hand? Figure that out and it will be okay. You will have difficulties in your marriage. Those plates will become unbalanced at times, but you can figure out how to add or remove a plate or two in order to achieve the proper balance. There will be difficult times, but talk to each other and adjust the stacks of plates. This is part of marriage. Do not let the unbalanced plates sway you. Just rebalance them.

> *Don't be proud at all. Be completely gentle. Be patient. Put up with one another in love. The Holy Spirit makes you one in every way. So try your best to remain as one. Let peace keep you together.* (Ephesians 4:2–3)

What difficulties does your marriage have right now, and how can you find peace and rebalance the plates?

Day 292

It is common in relationships, including marriages, that each person feels they do more than the other. My children tend to keep score—a tally sheet of what they do and what they receive. It is human nature. This is especially true in marriage. The ego keeps this tally sheet, but the true self is all love and does not care about the score. The true self does all things out of love. You love this person, so continue to do things for your spouse out of love. If you feel taken advantage of, realize that this is your ego. Your spouse loves you and does not want to take advantage of you.

> *[Love] keeps no record of wrongs.*
> (1 Corinthians 13:5 NIV)

Are you a scorekeeper? Is your spouse a scorekeeper? How can you get back to just being love?

Day 293

Marriage has difficult times because of the ego. When the ego flares up, it is important to squash it down and listen to the heart. At times, this can be difficult, but with My help and guidance, the heart will always prevail! The heart is the key to marriage, the root of love, the root of My love, and the root of Me. Being in the heart is not only the key to marriage, but it is the key to peace and happiness in life. The key is Me!

> *When pride comes, then comes disgrace, but with the humble is wisdom.* (Proverbs 11:2 ESV)

Do you listen to your heart or to your ego in your marriage? Why?

Day 294

When I am at the center, I am the key to lasting relationships. With Me at the center, marriages are able to survive many difficulties. Marriage is a commitment, not only to each other, but also to Me. Understand that you answer to Me and not just to your ego. Some people let their egos take over and only answer to themselves. When this happens, they are not doing what is best for the other person, but only for themselves. They have an inability to admit when they are wrong because the ego is telling them they are right. When they are ego-centered, they are unable to empathize with other people, for empathy comes from the heart. When they are able to step out of their egos and into their hearts, apologies occur. If people would stay out of the ego, and if they would love totally from the heart—with Me—then this world would be a much happier place.

> *But he gives more grace. Therefore it says, "God opposes the proud but gives grace to the humble."*
> (James 4:6 ESV)

Do you always think that you are right? Do you understand that it is your ego? Do you realize the damage that it causes in your relationships?

Day 295

It is all about communication. Through communication, you are able to work things out and then compromise. Compromise is very difficult for some people. Most people want to have things their own way. When you are in a relationship, you need to compromise. This is an important part of making a relationship work. If you do not ever want to compromise, then you reside in your ego, and you should not be in a relationship.

> *That's why a man leaves his father and mother and is joined to his wife. The two of them become one.* (Genesis 2:24)

Are both you and your spouse willing to compromise?

Day 296

Communication is one of the keys needed in relationships. It is not only needed in marriage, but it is also needed in life with family, children, and friends. If you are unable to communicate, your relationships will eventually fail. You also need to be able to put yourself in someone else's shoes and understand why that person acted the way they did. Then you need to come from the heart with empathy and understanding. You need to show them love. Remember to communicate with love and be empathetic.

> *There is one whose rash words are like sword thrusts,*
> *but the tongue of the wise brings healing.*
> (Proverbs 12:18 ESV)

With those whom you love, do you use your tongue like a weapon or with love?

Day 297

Learn to discuss issues right away, and do not let them fester. If you let them fester, you will become angry. However, if you talk about them right away with love and kindness, you are often able to diffuse the situation. Then the ego does not come out. Once the ego comes out, the situation will escalate and you will want to win. You will want your point to be made. When an ego "wins," nobody wins. The other person "loses," and no one really wins. Why would you want your spouse to lose? Come from a place of the heart, and squash the ego; that enables you both to win.

> *A fool takes no pleasure in understanding,*
> *but only in expressing his opinion.*
> (Proverbs 18:2 ESV)

Do you speak *at* your spouse or *to* your spouse? Is it your goal to problem-solve or to "win"?

CHAPTER 24

Judgmentalism and Gossip

Most people are good people
and do what they think is best.

God continually tells us that we are not to be judgmental toward other human beings, that it is He who is the judge of others. He lets us know that when we judge others, we are really unhappy with ourselves. We tend to point out flaws in others that are flaws in ourselves. Judgmentalism also leads to gossip. God lets us know that many times when we gossip about others, we are pointing out our own flaws. He wants us to understand that He knows us best and that we should let it go when others gossip about us. He constantly asks us not to be judgmental and gossip about others, but instead to love and lift each other up.

Day 298

This is a difficult topic. Everyone is judgmental. When you are judgmental with someone, it is because you are making yourself feel better about yourself. When you find what you think are flaws in another person, it makes you feel better about your own flaws. Remember this when someone is judgmental about you or others. Try not to take it personally. How can you become less judgmental? It is difficult to do, but realize that you are talking about one of My children. Also, if you understand why you are being judgmental, it will be easier to stop. Look for the positives in others and point those things out. Lift others up.

> *In the same way, the women must be worthy of respect. They must not say things that harm others. In anything they do, they must not go too far. They must be worthy of trust in everything.*
> (1 Timothy 3:11)

Do you find yourself being judgmental and saying harmful things about others? How can you lift that person up instead?

Day 299

Gossiping does no one any good. You are not to be judgmental about another person or their actions. That is reserved for Me and Me only. You never know someone else's story. You just don't know. Most people are good people and do what they believe is best. Everyone is brought up differently and sees things differently. Gossiping often makes you feel better about yourself.

> *Lord, guard my mouth.*
> *Keep watch over the door of my lips.*
> (Psalm 141:3)

Does gossiping make you feel better about yourself?

Day 300

When people gossip about others, they feel better about themselves. There will always be people who speak behind your back and gossip about you. Unfortunately, that is human nature. Look at the people doing this, and ask yourself if it really matters. Do you really care that they are gossiping about you? Understand that they are talking about you to feel better about themselves. Just let it go. I know you, and I know the person you are, so don't let it bother you when people gossip about you. I love you, and that is all that matters!

> *You are citizens together with God's people. You are also members of God's family.*
> (Ephesians 2:19)

Have people ever gossiped about you? Do you understand that God knows you and knows the person you are, so you should not concern yourself with their gossip? Is that difficult for you? Why?

CHAPTER 25

Who I Am

I am pure love.

Just who is God? God teaches us that He is pure love, nothing else. The Bible speaks continually of God's love for us. God loves us more than parents love their children. His love is so deep that our human minds are unable to fathom it. Did you know that God also has emotions? He feels sad when you are sad, and He is happy when you are happy. God teaches us that His love is pure.

Day 301

I am your Father, your Creator. I care about you more than anything or anyone in the world—so much so that you cannot fathom this. I know everything that has happened to you and that will happen to you. I am in charge of your life. I always want the best for you. There are times your choices do not end well, and then I am there for you, holding you and helping you to get through. I am a silent Father, watching until you call to Me for help. Just as with your child, you are silent until needed. Call to Me for help often. I allow you to make many choices, but if you surrender your life to Me, I will help you make the correct choices. I am love, pure love; there is no evil within Me.

> *Whoever confesses that Jesus is the Son of God,*
> *God abides in him, and he in God.*
> (1 John 4:15 ESV)

Can you even fathom that God is pure love? What does pure love mean?

Day 302

I am pure love—no evil, no ego, but simply pure love. Everything I think about is from true love. Do I have emotions? Yes. I experience sadness and anger. In humans, anger comes from the ego. I have anger because I am God. The way that I am is not the way that you are. Don't confuse Me with humans. You have a soul that is 100 percent love and is associated with all of your positive emotions, while the ego is associated with all of your negative emotions. I am pure love—100 percent love without an ego. I also experience anger and sadness, but in a loving way. Just as you get angry with your children, so I get angry with My children at times. Just as you have sadness with your children, so I experience sadness regarding My children at times. However, this comes from pure love, not from ego. I know this can be confusing to you, but remember that you have a human mind; you are not capable of totally understanding Me.

> *Jesus wept.*
> (John 11:35 NIV)

Did you know that God experiences emotion?

Day 303

Learn about Me. Learn to know the Me beyond Scripture—who I really am—a loving, kind, compassionate Father and friend. As your Father, I am not one whom you should be afraid of, but I am here to take away your fears, to love you, to hold you, and to help you solve your problems. I am a friend. In Me you have all the beautiful positives in life. See Me as your Father, your friend. You can laugh, joke, love, and even cry with Me. Do not have a fearful relationship with Me. My love for you is extreme. My love is so abounding and so deep that you cannot even begin to fathom the depth of My love for you.

> *I no longer call you servants, because a servant does not know his master's business. Instead, I have called you friends, for everything that I learned from my Father I have made known to you.* (John 15:15 NIV)

Just as you have gotten to know your friends here on Earth, what are some ways you can get to know God as a friend?

Day 304

My love for all of humanity, for all of My children, is greater than anyone can imagine. I love all of My children—even those who have strayed, like the Prodigal Son. I am always there to welcome them back with open arms. There are many distractions in today's world. People choose many things over Me, and that makes Me sad. But when those who have strayed come home, it is a cause for celebration. I am so happy! I am always excited when My children choose Me. Take the joy you would feel and multiply it exponentially.

> *"Let's have a feast and celebrate. For this son of mine was dead and is alive again; he was lost and is found." So they began to celebrate.*
> (Luke 15:23–24 NIV)

Do you let the distractions of this world take precedence over God?

Day 305

I will walk beside you. When you need directions, look to Me, and we will walk down the path together, side by side. During tough times, I will carry you. During joyous times, we will skip together through this wondrous life. We will walk together in joyfulness and peacefulness. So grab My hand, and let's skip through the next chapter of your life.

> *Draw near to God, and he will draw near to you.*
> (James 4:8 ESV)

Do you ask God to walk beside you, carry you, or even skip side by side with you through your life?

Day 306

You are My child, and I love you more than all others who love you combined. My love for you is deep! Nothing you can do will make Me love you any less. My love for you is beyond your comprehension. Feel My love for you. I feel all that you feel. When you are in pain, I am in pain. When you are happy, I am happy. My love for you is beyond your imagination—so much so that I have to let you make your own decisions, to let you be you. This is difficult for Me at times, especially when you make poor decisions, for I already know the pain it will cause you. However, I love you so much that I gave you freedom of choice. That is love, My child.

> *Consider the kind of extravagant love the Father has lavished on us—He calls us children of God! It's true; we are His beloved children. And in the same way the world didn't recognize Him, the world does not recognize us either.*
> (1 John 3:1 Voice)

Have you ever stopped to consider the great love that the Father must *feel* for us? He does not just *have* love for us, but He *feels* love for us!

Day 307

It always saddens Me to see My children sad. It breaks My heart. Remember, though, that each situation or event that brings sadness also brings growth in your life. It is an opportunity for you to become closer to Me, to strengthen your faith, and to make correct decisions about your life. There are always many positives to strife. It is just difficult to see the positives when you or a loved one are in the midst of the strife. Do not lose faith or let that loved one lose faith, for lessons will be learned. Look back upon this event and be grateful; one way or another it will be a good thing.

> *Jesus went forth, and saw a great multitude, and was moved with compassion toward them, and he healed their sick.* (Matthew 14:14 KJV)

Did you know that God is saddened by your sadness?

Day 308

Work hard to fortify your house. Continue to be with Me and I will always protect you. No matter what happens, I am with you; we will get through all of it together—you and Me! We are two peas in a pod, and the casing is My protective shield that protects you from all evil. This skin is getting thicker and stronger because of your strengthened faith and relationship with Me! Think of this skin when any evil comes toward you, and know that I will deflect any harm.

> *But the Lord is faithful, and he will strengthen you and protect you from the evil one.*
> (2 Thessalonians 3:3 NIV)

What evil has God protected you from in the past?

Day 309

When you are sick, I hear your prayer for healing. Just like so many things in life, this, too, takes time. It is like being sick with a cold and not knowing how much time it will take to feel better. It is the same with emotional healing; it just takes time. In today's society, people want things now. But healing doesn't often happen immediately. It is the same when you pray; it often just takes time to get the answer. I always answer your prayers. Sometimes I do not answer them in the way that you believe is best, but I always answer them in the way that I know is best!

> *"I will give perfect peace to those who are far away and those who are near. And I will heal them," says the* Lord. (Isaiah 57:19)

Are you impatient for healing when you are ill? Are you impatient for answers to your prayers? How can you develop more patience?

Day 310

I am always here to listen to you and to help you. I am your true Father who loves you more than you can ever imagine. I have been here holding you during your difficult times. Always feel My presence. When you need Me, I will be here holding you tightly. Never doubt that. Never believe that you were or are alone. I am here, and I always will be here. I promise you that!

> *The Lord is near to all who call on him, to all who call on him in truth.* (Psalm 145:18 ESV)

Do you understand that God is always here and has always been here? Do you understand that you have never been alone and never will be alone?

CHAPTER 26

Prayer

Prayers are always answered.

Have you ever thought that your prayers were not answered? God teaches us that all prayers are answered. They just might not be answered in the way that you think they should be answered. Sometimes the answer might just be no. Always remember, though, that God loves you because you are His child and He is your Father. He will answer your prayers in a way that is best for you. Sometimes these answers are in ways that you would have never thought possible, but always remember that God answers all of your prayers.

Day 311

I love it when My children pray to Me. They are speaking to their Father, asking for help, just as you would ask for help from your earthly father. As a Father, I know what is best for My children. Prayers are granted in the way that I know are best, just as an earthly father gives his children what he believes is best. Prayers are often answered in ways that are different than what you prayed for. This might cause you to believe that the prayer was not answered, but know that I answer all of your prayers.

> *Then they cried out to the LORD*
> *because of their problems.*
> *And he brought them out of their troubles.*
> (Psalm 107:28)

Do you believe that God hears your cries? Do you believe that He answers all of your prayers? Do you understand that many times the answer may not be the answer that you prayed for?

Day 312

I answer every prayer, although sometimes you might not know that I have answered it. The answer might not always be obvious to you, although sometimes it will be. Your prayers sometimes might not be answered in the way you think they should be answered, but your prayers are always answered.

> *If you believe, you will receive what you ask for when you pray.* (Matthew 21:22)

Are there some prayers that you have prayed that have left you uncertain as to whether or not God answered them? Are there some prayers that you have prayed that have received an obvious answer?

Day 313

Many people pray for healing. This prayer is always answered. Some people are healed physically, and some are not. Remember that all of you will die. When I grant healing, I am delaying someone's entry into heaven. You need to have faith that this person will be with Me. I understand why you pray for healing, but know that I will do what is best for all of My children, especially the ones who are ill. Sometimes the faith that healing brings for the person and the family and friends is so great that I will heal. Other times, it is more important for that person to come home to Me. Sometimes a person is healed by coming home to Me. Don't forget that when that happens, your prayer has been answered.

> *Trust in the Lord with all your heart and lean not on your own understanding.*
> (Proverbs 3:5 NIV)

Have you ever prayed for healing for a loved one and felt that the prayer was not answered? Did it ever occur to you that the prayer was answered when God brought that person home?

CHAPTER 27

The Soul

Love is the heart of the soul.

The soul is where God resides and is 100 percent love. Many people do their best to live in love, but many people also let their egos control their lives. As you have learned, the ego includes all the negatives—hate, greed, anger, jealousy—and the list goes on. Society praises those who live in their egos as opposed to those who live in their hearts. God tells us to live in our hearts, for the soul survives after death. The body is a vessel that contains the ego and the soul. When the body dies, so does the ego, but the soul goes home to be with God. Many people have experienced a time when they have surrendered their lives to God. Some call this total surrender, and others call it saving their souls. God is always there for you, but because we have free will, we need to grab on to God's hand and walk this journey with Him.

Day 314

Love is the heart of the soul. Everyone needs to be loved. Love is the nourishment of the soul. Food nourishes the body, and love nourishes the soul.

> *Truly my soul finds rest in God;*
> *my salvation comes from him.*
> (Psalm 62:1 NIV)

How often do you help others with love to nourish their souls? How often do you nourish your own soul?

Day 315

The ego is not part of the soul. The soul is the heart. The ego has no place in the heart, nor can it ever get there. Be careful, though, for the ego can cover the heart—and that is where many problems arise. The ego will begin to take over a person's actions. All of a sudden, a person is not acting from the soul/heart but from the ego.

> *A tranquil heart is life to the body,*
> *but passion is rottenness to the bones.*
> (Proverbs 14:30 NASB1995)

Do you understand the difference between the ego and the soul/heart?

Day 316

It is always nice to go home after a vacation. Home is where your roots are. It is a place of security and peacefulness. Vacations are an opportunity to get away, to see new places, and to see My beauty. As the saying goes, home is where the heart is, so after the vacation, you always want to go home. Just as when your body dies, your soul goes home. It longs to come home to Me. That longing that you felt to go home after a vacation is the same longing your soul feels to come home to Me. There is a draw in everyone from the soul to come home to Me.

> *God, you are my God.*
> *I seek you with all my heart.*
> *With all my strength I thirst for you*
> *in this dry desert*
> *where there isn't any water.*
> (Psalm 63:1)

Did you know that your soul thirsts to go home to God?

Day 317

For many people, the pull of the earthly world is so great that it overshadows the pull of the soul to Me. Another way to say it is that when the ego takes over, the soul/heart still longs to come home to Me, but the ego's longing for earthly things is stronger. It is a pendulum. For some people, the pull of earthly things is so great that they lose sight of the pull to Me. Always let your soul pull you to Me. Squash the ego enough to let My light shine in your soul to regenerate and strengthen it. Many people do not realize this struggle because their egos have gotten so strong, but I just need one crack in the ego so I can nourish and strengthen the soul.

> *I can do nothing by myself. I judge only as I hear. And my judging is fair. I do not try to please myself. I try to please the one who sent me.*
> (John 5:30)

Can you feel your soul longing for God?

Day 318

Be faithful, be kind, and let others see Me in you—by your heart and by your love. I reside in your heart, and that is where your soul is. Since I am pure love and I am in your heart, doesn't that let you know, then, that the soul has to be all love? Whenever you act with love, you are acting from your soul. My will for you is to always act from your soul, and that, then, is a reflection of Me—of love. Live by love.

> *Therefore be imitators of God, as beloved children; and walk in love, just as Christ also loved you and gave Himself up for us, an offering and a sacrifice to God as a fragrant aroma.* (Ephesians 5:1–2 NASB1995)

Do you now understand why your soul is pure love?

Day 319

I gave you freedom of choice. The ego influences many of your decisions. When you make a poor choice or when you sin, it is recorded on your soul. Imagine it like a cut on your soul. It will heal through My forgiveness, but you need to ask for forgiveness. I have given you the sacraments to heal your soul. Take advantage of them.

> *While they were eating, Jesus took bread. He gave thanks and broke it. He handed it to his disciples and said, "Take this and eat it. This is my body."*
>
> *Then he took a cup. He gave thanks and handed it to them. He said, "All of you drink from it. This is my blood of the covenant. It is poured out to forgive the sins of many people."*
> (Matthew 26:26–28)

One of the sacraments that Christ provided for us is Communion. When is the last time you took advantage of this sacrament?

Day 320

Many of My children have a glorious moment when they decide to let Me save their soul from darkness. It is a moment when they choose their soul over their current situation. They often do not realize it until later—sometimes years later. It is a preservation of the soul. You know that you are about to fall into the abyss and that it will take a miracle to stop the fall—the miracle of Me. My hand reaches down into the abyss, but you still have to make the choice to grab My hand. The epiphany is when you make that choice and grab My hand.

> *Everyone who calls on the name of the Lord will be saved.* (Romans 10:13 ESV)

Have you ever had that moment when you felt that you needed to make the decision to ask God to save your soul? If so, when was it and how did it feel? What beautiful things happened after you grabbed God's hand?

CHAPTER 28

Perfection

I alone am perfect, but you should strive for perfection in your love of others.

Do you try to be perfect in your life and in your relationships? God teaches us that no one is perfect and that we should not expect perfection from others. If you do, you will be disappointed. The only perfection on Earth is God, and it is human for us to make mistakes. God teaches us to forgive ourselves for the mistakes that we make and also to forgive others for their mistakes. Being perfect is unrealistic, and trying to be so causes issues in many relationships. God asks us to learn from our mistakes and to understand that we are not perfect!

Day 321

Only I am perfect. Stop trying to make your life perfect. It is impossible to do so. Relationships will never be perfect. They can be good, fruitful, loving, and joyous, but not perfect. Enjoy every moment—even those that are not perfect.

> *Am I now trying to get people to think well of me? Or do I want God to think well of me? Am I trying to please people? If I were, I would not be serving Christ.* (Galatians 1:10)

If we know that God accepts us as we are, who are we trying to be perfect for?

Day 322

I know that you are not perfect. Only I am perfect. However, strive to be excellent in your love of others. Strive for perfection in being kind to your neighbors—especially those who are your "enemies." This is very difficult to do. It is easy to love those who love you, but it is difficult to love those who do not love you. This is where I want you to strive for perfection. Love your enemies. When you love your enemies, people will see Me in you.

> *But I tell you, love your enemies and pray for those who persecute you.* (Matthew 5:44 NIV)

Do you find it difficult to love your "enemies"? How can you get better at this?

Day 323

Everyone fails at some point. You are not perfect; only I am. It is good for you to know that you will fail and have failed. That is okay. Expect others to fail too. It is part of life.

> *Jeremiah, tell them, "The LORD says, 'When people fall down, don't they get up again? When someone turns away, don't they come back?'"* (Jeremiah 8:4)

Do you understand that failing is a part of life?

Day 324

You are not perfect. No human is. That is My job. Don't beat yourself up when you fail, for it is through failing that you learn and get better. If you never fail, how will you learn?

> *Even if godly people fall down seven times, they always get up.* (Proverbs 24:16)

Think about the last time you fell down and got back up. How did God help you?

Day 325

You tend to expect others to be perfect. You think that relationships will be perfect. You must realize that no one is perfect. No one except Me can live up to perfection. Once you realize this, it will be easier for you to accept people and situations when they are not perfect. Do not expect a relationship to be perfect. Do not expect another person to be perfect. When you do, you are setting that situation or that person up for failure.

> *And He has said to me, "My grace is sufficient for you, for power is perfected in weakness." Most gladly, therefore, I will rather boast about my weaknesses, so that the power of Christ may dwell in me.* (2 Corinthians 12:9 NASB1995)

Do you set up others for failure in your quest for perfection?

Day 326

You are a wonderful child of Mine, but you are not perfect—and that is okay. I love you despite your imperfections. Everyone makes mistakes. Why? Because no one is perfect except Me. Forgive yourself when you fail, just as Jesus forgives you. It is through imperfections that you are able to be closer to Me. It is through imperfections that you learn. If you were perfect, how would you learn? Accept your imperfections. Let them remind you that only I am perfect.

> *Suppose we claim we are without sin. Then we are fooling ourselves. The truth is not in us. . . . If we claim we have not sinned, we are calling God a liar. His word is not in us.* (1 John 1:8, 10)

Who is someone from whom you can remove your expectation of perfection? Yourself? Your spouse? Your child? A friend?

CHAPTER 29

Analogies

I am the fertilizer of the soul.

God has always given me analogies to help me understand His teachings. I have included many in the previous reflections, but I wanted to share some more in this section. Some of these are longer than others, but they all are worth your time to read and reflect upon. I am always amazed at the teachings that God gives me, and I hope they impact you as much as they have impacted me!

Day 327

CROWDED ROOM

It is as if we are in a crowded room and you can't see Me. I am there, but there are so many other people in the way—in between us. You have to sort through and walk past all these people to find Me. Stop inviting all these people over. They are taking up the space in the room. Slowly you have asked them to leave. Some are more stubborn than others. Finally, you can see Me over in the corner! Come to Me. Let the others go. It will be just our party—just you and Me!

Is God in a crowded room in your life? Do you have any space left for God?

Day 328

FRUIT TREES

Look around you during the next few months and see My glory in people. Notice how people change when they walk with Me. Watch their growth and love change. Watch their faith grow—like a seedling that has been planted and cultivated. It is beginning to sprout, but keep those weeds out of the way; help pull the weeds. As the sprout grows, it gets stronger, growing into a mature plant. People gain more and more strength as their faith in Me grows. At some point, a blossom will appear, but even this blossom must be fertilized. I am the fertilizer of the soul. Soon the blossom bears fruit—the product of faith in Me. Our faith and love together bear this glorious fruit. What was once a fragile sapling has become a glorious fruit tree.

Some of the flowers will not blossom. Some will wither away, some will bear sour fruit, and some will bear no fruit at all. These were not fertilized by faith in Me. Fruit will fall to the ground and create new saplings. Some will turn into glorious new fruit trees, while others will not. This is how it works with people. Some saplings will grow into fruit-bearing trees and will spread their fruit to others. Some will just wither and die, and others will grow and never produce fruit. With faith and with Me as the fertilizer, all will bear glorious fruit. It is all about the fertilizer. It is all about Me. It takes both of us to make the fruit. May our relationship of love and faith continue to grow!

What type of tree are you? Do you produce fruit? Do you cultivate others? Do you allow God to fertilize your soul?

Day 329

CATERPILLAR

Allowing others to make their own choices can be difficult as a parent. You want to help your kids with their decisions. I watch My children make poor decisions every day, and it is tough. Don't take away their freedom of choice though. I did not take it away from you, so don't you take it away from your children or from others in your life. When you control, you are taking their freedom of choice away. Do you see that? If you pick up a caterpillar that is crossing a sidewalk and put it on the other side, you are taking away its freedom of choice—not on purpose, but nonetheless, you are taking it away. The caterpillar needs to make many choices before it can become a butterfly and fly away. If it makes the right choices, a metamorphosis happens and it becomes a butterfly. So let the caterpillars in your life make their own choices. They will either fly or they won't, but it is their choice. It can be difficult to let them make their own decisions, especially when the choice is obviously wrong in your eyes—but it may be the right choice for them. They may need to learn a lesson before moving on. Give your children the opportunity to learn the lessons they need to learn so that they, too, can learn to fly someday.

Do you try to control the decisions of others? Do you now understand that you have to let others make their own decisions so that they can fly?

Day 330

MOUNTAIN CLIMB

It takes time and much effort to get back to Me once you have drifted far from Me. It is like climbing a mountain: it is difficult to get to the top, but it is very easy to slip and fall. If you slip and roll down the mountain, then you have to hike back up through the trees and boulders to get to the top. Use Me as your lifeline. Follow the rope I give you, and I will guide you and pull you up. When you have difficulty, call to Me. I will tug the rope and help pull you along. Soon you will get above the tree line, but you may get stuck in snow. Continue to call to Me. I will pull you up and provide sunshine for the rest of your trip. Don't slip on the ice or get stuck in the deep snow. Continue to climb upward. The view is so beautiful and peaceful up here with Me.

Where are you on the mountain? Are you sliding down? Are you climbing up? Are you near the top? Do you ever call to God for help in your journey with Him?

Day 331

COMMUNICATION WITH GOD

Picture our conversations as if they are similar to cell-phone service. There are times when the connection is crystal clear, there are times when there is static, and there are still other times when there is dead space. Static occurs when your space is filling up. If you don't move back into the clear space, you will enter into a hole and lose total contact with Me. The good news is that when you get out of the hole, you can call Me back. But while you are in the hole, you cannot reach Me. So how do you stay connected? You stay connected by keeping space for Me, by surrendering to Me.

The difference between cell-phone service and Me is that you have the control to keep the lines open with Me through surrender and space. You can stay close to the cell-phone tower. The more that comes between you and the cell-phone tower, the more static there is, and soon there is dead space and a loss of connection. So keep the space between you and the cell-phone tower clear. Keep the line of communication open.

What type of cell-phone service do you have with God? Is it clear? Is there a lot of static? Are you in a dead space? Is your line of communication open to God? If not, why not? How can you change this?

Day 332

ORCHESTRA

Everything is orchestrated by Me. From the simple clanging of symbols to the banging of drums to the beauty of a flute, it is all orchestrated by Me. But as you know, some symphonies or songs take longer to compose than others. Some parts of the symphony are more complicated than others, but in the end, there is a beautiful song to be played. It takes many instruments to play the symphony. Each part, no matter how small, is important to the entire song. Sometimes a player does not get to the part of the symphony right away where he gets to play, but ultimately, the conductor who puts the piece together makes sure everyone is playing their part.

Where are you in your symphony of life with God? Are you in the beginning? The middle? The end? Do you understand that some parts of your life take longer to orchestrate, but that in the end, your life is a beautiful symphony conducted by God?

Day 333

ANTS

Look at an anthill. There are so many ants running around. Few are going into the center of the anthill. They are all looking for something. When they find it, they go to the center, down the hole to the nest. So many of My children are running around looking and searching, and then they finally find Me and head home. However, many people never find Me. Many people do not make it home. They get lost along the way, still searching and not finding Me.

Are you like an ant running all over the place chaotically looking for something? Do you realize you are searching for God? Do you see many other people running around searching for God? What can you do to help them?

Day 334

RAFT LESSON

Look at the strength of a river, as well as the beauty in the stillness of the water; just as life is, it seems chaotic at times, but it always flows downhill toward Me. Even in the calmness of the water, it is still flowing toward Me. However, there are times when a raft will get stuck among the rocks or trees and will fight to get free but remains stuck. A determined person will be able to free the raft. He will free himself and continue onward toward Me. It may take some strength and determination, but the ride will be beautiful and glorious. It will be exciting at times and calm at times, but never forget to look at the beauty of the race! At the end, the river meets its destination as it flows into the ocean. Notice how the Guide (Me) knows how to navigate the waters. I make going down the river so much easier. Notice how you go over the rapids almost effortlessly. If you do not follow Me, you will have the uncertainty of each rapid, the concern of having no direction, and the fear of getting stuck. So just ride down the river with Me—to heaven.

Where are you on your raft journey? Are you stuck in the rocks? Are you going over rapids? Are you in calm waters? Do you see how much easier it is to go on this ride with God as the guide?

Day 335

BUSH

With each failure comes new growth. It is like pruning a bush. As a bush grows, it needs to be pruned and shaped. As the bush continues to grow, more shaping and pruning are needed. Sometimes bushes are never shaped or pruned and just grow out of control. Branches are growing this way and that. But that bush can still be shaped and pruned at any time. It will take much work as the bush will need to be pruned back considerably to get a beautiful shape. Throughout the life of the bush, branches will still need to be pruned. Some branches will die and will need to be cut away, but after they are cut, the bush will be even more beautiful. Such is life. Results of the ego need to be cut away, and sometimes these branches are very thick and long. As they are cut away, new life is breathed into the bush. Let Me be the gardener in your life to shape and prune you. Remember, though, that one pruning does not last forever. It is a continual process!

Do you need to be shaped and pruned by God?

Day 336

FISHING POLE

When you are drifting or have drifted from Me, you need to be reeled back in. Just as with fishing, the current will pull the line out, and then the fisherman needs to reel the line back in. Then the current will pull it back out, and when it is too far away, the fisherman will need to reel it back in. This occurs over and over again. When the current pulls you too far from Me, let Me reel you back. I am the fisherman, and you are the line. Do not let the line snap or get caught up in the rocks or twigs. When the line is caught up in these, I will pull you back, but sometimes the line still gets snagged on a rock. Break loose from the rock and let Me pull you back. Try to avoid the snags of the brush, but if you end up in the brush, call to Me to wiggle the line to free you. Our journey together can be smooth, so don't get caught up in the strong currents of life. When the waters get rough, let Me reel you back.

Are you caught up in the current and drifting away from God? Do you call to Him to pull you back toward Him? How can you make your journey smoother?

Day 337

MIRROR

Many people look in a mirror that is covered with the fingerprints of the ego. Some fingerprints will be stubborn and will be difficult to clean off. Let Me clean off the fingerprints and make the mirror shiny and clear. Other people may come and add fingerprints or smudges to your mirror. This is life. This is ego—always adding fingerprints or smudges to mirrors. It is a constant battle to keep the mirror clean, but when it is clean, your true self is revealed. Just as other people add smudges and fingerprints to your mirror, there are people who help Me clean your mirror, just as you can help others clean their mirrors.

When many people look in the mirror, all they see is a blur of their true self. They do not even know that the mirror is blurry. Be patient with these people. Help them to see their true self. Help them to clear the smudges and fingerprints one at a time. Help them to see the beauty of their true self. It is only when fingerprints are cleared that they can see the world clearly. Don't let other people add smudges and fingerprints to your mirror. Work with Me to keep your mirror clean so you can see your true self. This is part of the journey. This is the journey to the true self without ego.

What does your mirror look like? Is it full of fingerprints? Are you willing to clean them off with God so you can see your true self more clearly?

Day 338

TRAIN

You had a little derailment recently, but you are back on track, You had a few bumps on the track, and they continued to get worse. Instead of changing tracks, you continued on the bumpy track, and soon your train was derailed. It happened so easily and quickly. Learn to let Me smooth down the bumps before they get so large that your train derails. Also, teach others to let Me smooth the bumps on their tracks and get their trains back on the tracks. How? Through Me and only Me. This can be difficult, but when there is a will, there is a way. Help others to see the path and get back on the track!

Do you have bumps on your train track? Are they small ones or large ones? Has your train been derailed? How can you get back on the track?

Day 339

SPARKLING WATER

Looking out at the ocean, I can see a huge group of sparkles in the water. They dissipate as they get farther from the center. What does this mean?

The multitude of sparkles are all of My sheep that have come home and have the sparkle of light showing in their hearts. They are all gathered around Me in the center. As you move away from the center, the sparkles become less evident. These are the ones on the outside looking in who are searching for Me. Their light is dimmer than the ones surrounding Me. They are looking and searching for Me, but the tide is pulling them away. These are the ones who need My help. They need to come home so they can be with Me. I am reaching out for them, but they are not able to grab on to My hand. Those who are with Me need to reach out their hands to make a train to help pull them to Me. Be one of those helping hands—a hand that is linked to My hand. Lengthen the bridge to help them grab on to Me. Help pull them to Me against the tide so they, too, will become a part of the group to further lengthen the human chain that leads to Me.

Where are you in the sparkling water? Are you near the center? Are you on the outskirts? How bright is your light? Are you allowing the tide to pull you away from God? Do you keep your hand outstretched for God and for others?

Day 340

BAGGAGE

Everyone has baggage. It is just a part of life. Some people are able to lay it down when it gets slightly heavy. Others try to prove their strength and carry it until they actually fall over. Which are you? Are you the one who feels that you have to prove your strength and carry it, even adding more baggage? Do you often even carry other people's baggage? You will learn that this does not work. You will eventually fall and become so weakened by the weight that you cannot go on. It may take this incredible weight for you to finally turn to Me and give Me your baggage. But then what happens? You eventually start picking up more baggage. This is human nature, especially for one of strength. But is this really strength? Actual strength comes from giving Me your baggage and trusting Me. This can be very difficult. Give Me one small bag at first, and feel your burden lightened. Then trust Me with a larger, heavier bag, and finally with all your bags.

How much baggage do you carry? Are you someone who does not just carry your own baggage but also the baggage of others? What baggage can you give God today?

Day 341

SOLAR PANELS

All day long when the sun is shining, power is being brought into your home. All day long you are given so many blessings. In fact, you have so many blessings that you cannot hold them all. This is just like the solar power to your home. During the day, there is too much power for your house. Some of the power is sent to the backup battery, and the excess is sent out to the world. It is the same with you and Me. All day long you are given many blessings—so many that you might not even see all of them. Put some of them, then, in your backup battery. There are still more! Send the rest out to the world, just as your excess solar power goes out to the world.

When darkness comes, you use your battery power, and some of the power that was sent out to the grid is returned to you. It is the same with you. When a storm or darkness comes, you might need to use your "battery," and if this is not enough, you are able to get some of the power back that you sent out into the world. There are also some days that are extremely sunny. On those days, you see your blessings in abundance. Other days are cloudy or stormy. On these days, you might not notice your blessings. It is on these days that you can rely on the battery power or the power that you had sent out to the world by way of your family, your friends, the church, and of course Me. Ultimately, you get power from Me. The power you send out is the help you give others. The power you receive may not necessarily come from the same people to whom you gave your power, but it will come.

Do you see your blessings on a sunny day? On a cloudy day? On a stormy day? Do you send out blessings to others?

Day 342

CLEAR WATER VERSUS MURKY WATER

We need our channel to be wide open and clear, like a river that is so clear that you can see the riverbed. Otherwise, there is much debris that muddies the water. When this happens, you can't hear Me clearly. Let's always work to keep our river clear and free of debris, to keep our channel of communication open without interference. Do you understand the importance of this? I don't like it when it's blocked, so always do your best to keep our channel open and get rid of the muck. When you allow things to get in the way, you are allowing muck in your life—slimy, dark, smelly, disgusting muck. Look at it this way: When things get in the way, filter out all the muck so the water is clear again. The debris pollutes our relationship, so don't let the debris get in the way!

What is your river like? Is it wide open? Is it narrow? Is it clear? Is it murky? How much debris is in your river? How can you clear it out?

Day 343

EMOTIONAL SCAR

The scar will always be there; the wound is just seeping. Someday, the seeping will stop and you will just have a scar—a badge of honor. This was a deep wound, and deep wounds take a long time to heal. They fester periodically, but eventually they heal. So this is just a wound that is seeping. Let's add some ointment (Me) that will help it to heal.

Do you have an emotional scar that just won't heal—one that keeps on seeping? Are you willing to let God help heal this wound?

Day 344

SURRENDER/BOXING MATCH

When you accept where things are, when you accept what they are, and when you accept the fact that you cannot change them, it is then that you come to acceptance. Once you have acceptance, you can surrender these things. Sometimes you keep surrendering things, and then you keep taking them back. You need to have total surrender and total acceptance. Accept that I am in control and that you are not. You are trying to fight a fight that is not yours to fight. It is as if you are watching a boxing match and throwing punches while sitting on the outside of the ring. Your punches are not landing on anything but are just catching air. You are exhausted and discouraged by the fight, but you are not even in the fight. Accept that you are not in this fight and that you have no bearing on the outcome. Let Me do the fighting while you work on acceptance and surrender. Remember that you are only a spectator, not a boxer. There are unexpected punches in boxing, and many times the underdog will win. I am the secret weapon—the knockout punch that is unexpected. So watch the fight and know that love is protected from the evil.

Do you ever feel as if you are a spectator outside the boxing ring fighting a fight that is not yours to fight? Are you trusting enough to let God be the secret weapon?

Day 345

FOG

Sometimes the fog needs to lift in order for you to see things more clearly. Just like when you drive in the fog, you can only see a few feet in front of you. You have to concentrate. You have to be in the present. When the fog lifts, you can see clearly, and you see the gifts and blessings of the fog. Without the fog, you cannot and will not see the blessings of the clear road. Many people walk around in fog and are never able to see the clear road. They walk around in despair and hopelessness, being victims. They never surrender. They never allow the fog to lift, so they never see the beautiful path and their blessings. I want you to know that despite difficulties, the sun does shine and will shine again.

Are you living your life in the present or in the future? Are you spending your life walking around in the fog?

Day 346

THE LITTLE ENGINE THAT COULD

Doesn't it feel better to let Me carry your burdens? You tend to try to help fix other people's problems, but you have learned that, in many cases, you cannot fix them; only I can. You still take on these heavy burdens though. You are not strong enough to carry them all, but I've got to hand it to you—you have perseverance. You are like the engine in *The Little Engine that Could*, except that your engine is not strong enough for the load you are carrying. The hill is too steep. It is so steep that you are falling backward and slipping down the hill. I will come and pull you up the hill. Trust that I am fixing all of these problems. In the meantime, I will take the heavy cargo cars off the train so your load is lighter!

Are you like the little engine that could? Are you trying to carry not only your own burdens but also those of others? How can you release them to God?

Day 347

WAVES

I know that life can be exhausting with one wave coming after another, but look how strong you are with Me by your side. Those waves will not knock you down, rush over you, and pull you into the sea. Your legs may get wobbly, but you will not fall! I know you are tired from being battered by the waves, but low tide is on the way. Just hang in there. I'm here with a raft for you so you can rest your weary legs. Hop on board and let Me hold the raft steady while you rest! Soon it will be low tide, and you can rest in the water and feel the waves—refreshing waves, soft waves, clean waves—upon your face. The clouds are parting, and the sun is beginning to peek through.

Do you ever feel as if you are being battered by the waves of life? How does it feel to know that low tide always comes and that God will give you a raft to rest your weary legs if you surrender to Him? How does it feel to know that sunshine will be coming?

Day 348

BUS/STUDENTS

Notice where your journey is now. Is this where you want to be? Have you chosen to get off the bus before you reach the top of the mountain? The road is pretty high. Some of you will get off partway up the mountain, some will get off most of the way up the mountain, and some of you will make it all the way to the top. That's okay, because I am happy that you are on the bus! I am your bus driver, and I always want you to ride to the top of the mountain, but if you don't, I am still thrilled that you got on the bus!

Where are you on the mountain? Do you want to go higher? What is your first step in moving higher?

Day 349

SEASONS

The Easter season reflects winter and spring—from the "death" of Christ to the "awakening" and "rebirth" of Christ. Let's look at all the seasons. Christ is born in the summertime—there is so much joy and healing and learning about Me. There is so much love all around! There is so much hope! Then autumn comes and the "fall." The hate begins. Things are off. The trees lose their leaves. Then comes winter. Snow blankets the earth. The coldness is felt throughout—the crucifixion—the ultimate deep freeze. Then it is spring. It is no secret that Easter is in the springtime. It is the time of Christ's resurrection, the beginning of life, and the beginning of the church. It is such a time of rebirth and new life. The birds are chirping, singing of the resurrection and the birth of Christ. It is such a joyous time.

Have you ever thought to compare Jesus' death and resurrection to the seasons? Does it help you to understand?

Day 350

PATH

I know that within your heart you are absolutely striving to be a better person. I know this is difficult, and all I ask is that you put your best foot forward, that you are continually moving forward in your journey. This is not to say that you won't stumble or take a few steps back at times. That's okay. I am here to move you forward. I am your personal traffic cop, always directing you down the safe path, the right path, with Me. There are times when difficulties will try to steer you off the path. Follow the orange cones to safety. Follow the smooth road. I will always lead you down the clear path. It is the ego that pulls you to the wrong path. Sometimes you are off the path before you even know it. Don't fret. I will be there to direct you back. You will face many struggles, but when you stay with Me, the struggles are easier. So be with Me and stay on the road with Me!

Thinking of God as a traffic cop, do you need to follow His orange cones to get you on the right path?

Day 351

BUMPS OF LIFE

Many roads are bumpy, but in the end, trust your faith. Trust in Me. I am here to help you get through these difficulties. I will smooth out the bumps, and you will ride over them with Me to heaven. That is truly glorious! Try to enjoy the bumps. They are the spice of life. Look at them as faith-building bumps. Each one is an opportunity to surrender and build faith. Faith is like all-terrain tires. You need to let Me put them on for you, and the ride will be smoother and easier. Trust in Me, have faith in Me, and surrender each bump, both large and small, to Me. You can look back and reflect on your life and the bumps and see how I have smoothed them out for you. You can also look at the faith you have built from each of these.

Do you allow the bumps in your life to strengthen your faith? Do you understand that without these bumps, you would not have the opportunities to build your faith?

Day 352

BATTLE

Think of good versus evil as the front lines of a battle. Each side moves toward the other. Sometimes evil gets the upper hand and moves the battle line. Then the good side pushes forward and moves the battle line back. This can represent the constant battles in your life. Battles might continually come into your camp, and you need to keep pushing them out further and further. You will win this battle and this war. I know it may be a long, hard-fought war, but peace and love will win out! I know your troops may get tired, but soon you will have rest. Dig deep down to your heart, and peace will win out. It always does. I know there are times when it does not seem that way, but it will! It always will! Hang tough with Me. You will win the war, and I will give you strength to move forward and carry on.

Does it seem as if the evil in your life and all around you is winning? How do you handle this? Do you have the faith to know that God and love will always prevail?

Day 353

DIAMOND

Trust Me with the things in your life, just as if you were letting Me hold on to a diamond. Would you trust Me with a valuable stone? Imagine the largest diamond in the world. Would you trust Me with it? Would you trust Me to hold on to the diamond and shape it accordingly—to cut each facet and make it shine brilliantly? I will do this with your entire life. Don't let others try to cut the facets, for then the diamond will end up dull and less brilliant. Do not think that you are a master cutter, either. You might think you are, but you are not. Let Me cut the diamond! Let Me make it shine brilliantly. Each situation is just one facet in your life. It may be a complicated corner of the stone to cut. That is all the more reason for you to allow the Master to cut it—right? Your brilliant light inside will then shine and reflect even more brilliantly. Those who allow Me to cut and shape their stones into diamonds shine the brightest of all!

Do you trust God in all facets of your life? Do you allow Him to shape and mold you into a brilliant diamond? If not, why not?

Day 354

ASPEN LEAF: PART 1

God, looking at the aspen tree outside the window, I see one leaf that is so much larger than the others, and my eye keeps going to it. Why?

Isn't nature wonderful? There are so many lessons to be taught by nature. Yes, that leaf is so much larger. What made it larger? Perfect sun, perfect rain, and perfect wind. Everything for that particular leaf was perfect. This leaf is how I want them all to be—larger than life—but things are not always perfect. So many have the same sunlight, rain, and wind, but they are not as large. Look at the tree. Only one large leaf is like that. I want all of My children to be the large leaf, but many are stunted by the problems of the world. They do not have enough rain or sun, or they have too much wind. Their growth is stunted. Those who take in the sun and rain grow stronger and larger than others. Yes—the sun and rain are Me. Those who take Me in and let Me nourish them will grow bigger and stronger. Those who do not will not grow as large. Be the large leaf on the tree. Let Me be your nourishment.

How can you take more of God within you to allow Him to nourish you?

Day 355

ASPEN LEAF: PART 2

God, looking at the aspen tree from yesterday, I see that a few of the leaves are now bigger. Yesterday, I only saw one large leaf. Today there are several more.

This happened so I could teach you. Yesterday there was only one large leaf, and today there are several, all on the same branch. It is the spreading of My Word—the spreading of Me! It starts with just one person who shares with another and grows. Then that person shares with someone else who grows, and so forth. Soon a tree is filled with many large leaves. Notice that not all of the leaves on the branch are big. The smaller leaves are those that have chosen not to gather all the sunlight and rain. Those that do make the choice to flourish. Be the large leaf that made the choice originally, and then make the choice to share with others. Some will make the choice to join you and flourish, and others will not.

Do you want to become a larger leaf? What choices are you making to flourish? Are those around you small leaves or large leaves? Are you willing to help other leaves grow?

Day 356

GOLF

God, I played well on the first nine holes and so horribly on the back nine holes. I'm sure there is a lesson in all of this.

This golf game is just like life. You were doing so well, and then it took a turn for the worse and continued to go downhill. You played worse and worse to the point that you could not even believe how badly you were playing. That was the worst nine holes you have ever played. You were doing your best to remain positive, but it was so difficult to be positive when things were so bad. You were upset and angry, confused and saddened, but you could not do anything to make it better. You even had a few good shots and thought to yourself, *Okay, this is getting better*—but then more bad shots followed. You could not figure out how to fix it. You were so relieved when the game was over. You were almost joyous!

That is what it feels like when you are dealing with a difficult situation in your life. You are finishing up a bad game. You will be tired and spent from the game, but you will play again. In life, there will be some bad games, some bad holes, and some bad shots, but as you walk with Me and practice, your game will get better. When life lessons are to be learned, you might feel as if your life is going downhill for a bit. Just like when you change your golf swing, your game gets worse for a while before it gets better. You must have patience as you learn the new swing. You are now learning about being present and having faith in Me. You will need to practice this until it becomes habit, but this will help perfect your game!

Do you sometimes feel that your life is like a bad round of golf? Where can you take lessons to learn how to perfect your swing?

Day 357

CLAUDE MONET

Have you ever looked at Claude Monet's art? Notice in his paintings that what looks like chaos up close appears beautiful from farther away. This is so similar to life. When you are focusing on one part, one small piece, there may appear to be chaos, but when you stand back, you see the beautiful piece of art—your life!

Are you familiar with Claude Monet's artwork? Have you ever stood close to one of his paintings and thought that it just looked like paint strokes? Then when you stepped back, you saw that it was beautiful artwork. Can you see how this relates to life? Do you ever get too focused on one part of your life and forget about the rest of your life? Do you ever take the time to stand back and look at your beautiful life and see all of the blessings, or do you tend to focus on the chaos?

Day 358

SNOW

The symbolism is beautiful. Look at the freshness of snow. Look at its purity. It is untouched by anything. There are no footsteps, no dirt—nothing. It is very pure and white. As the day goes along, people walk and drive on it and it becomes dirty. Such is life. Purity is tainted by humans, but then it snows again, wiping away the impurity—and it becomes fresh and white again. Be with Me, and let's make your snow white and pure!

Have you ever noticed how pure and clean the world looks after a new snowfall? Have you ever noticed how dirty the snow becomes after a few days? Do you see this in your life? Do you allow God to make your snow fresh and pure again?

Day 359

SNOWFLAKES

When you look at all the different snowflakes, you can see that each one is different and yet equally beautiful. I see each of these as I see My children. They are so uniquely different, yet so beautiful. You are on Earth for such a short time, just as the snowflake is before it melts and turns into water. Your lives are the same. Your bodies will return to the earth, except that your souls will come home to Me.

Have you ever really looked at a snowflake up close and noticed its beauty? Do you see the correlation to God's children?

Day 360

BUCKET

A bucket can only hold so much water. Once it is full, it overflows. It is the same with you. You have been filling your bucket with many large burdens, and now it is overflowing. This is human nature. Now you need to empty the bucket. How? Let Me drink the water. Let Me take the burdens. Jesus drank all of your sins, so let go of everything. Hand it all over to Me.

What burdens have you recently put into your bucket? Is your bucket overflowing?

Day 361

SAND BUNKER

God, today I saw a sand bunker on the golf course that was covered in geese footprints. It was so beautiful!

Individually, at first glance, the footprints looked like confusion, but when you stepped away, you saw a beautiful design. This is just like life. At times, your life may look like confusion, moving this way and that way, but in the end, you find your way. There are also times when you do not know which way to turn. You may have felt confused at the time, but now you can look back and see how these events contributed to the beautiful design of your life. In your life, each episode, each page, and each chapter may seem to be in chaos, but each is perfectly placed to make the beautiful picture.

Do you often feel like your life is full of confusion? Do you not know which way to turn? Do you feel as if you turned the wrong way? Can you see that this is just part of the beautiful design of your life?

Day 362

LETDOWN/MOUNTAIN/VALLEY

Many people experience a feeling of letdown after a positive and exciting experience, like a wedding or a trip. But letdown can also happen after a tragedy. Your adrenaline only works for so long. You need to learn to live again, to start anew, without the heavy burden. This is like being at the bottom of a hill. You look around and are not sure what to do next. Do you climb the next hill or just hang out in the valley? There does not seem to be much excitement in the valley. It is pretty calm. You are used to the adrenaline rush of climbing up or going downhill. That is letdown. This is a time to regroup and to get supplies for the next hill, the next climb. It is also a time to rest. There is often a feeling of melancholy because of the lack of excitement. Use this time to rest your weary bones and rejuvenate. Don't lose sight of the beauty of calmness. Enjoy the letdown. Enjoy the peace, for the next climb is just around the corner.

When is the last time you experienced a letdown? Did you use it as a time to rejuvenate, or were you just looking for the next adrenaline rush?

Day 363

RACE

Peace is a time to revitalize yourself and rest. Just like training for a marathon, you work so hard every day training and eating right. Then comes the race. You run it, and you are exhausted afterward. Then you begin to recover. There is a time afterward when you need to rest. You feel as if you should be doing something, but there is nothing to do. This is how it is with peace. There are times when you are in constant worry and stress. It had become a part of who you are. Then suddenly, the stress and worry are gone. It seems weird, as if you should be doing something, anything. This is the time to relax your weary body and recuperate before the training for the next race. This time is just as important as training. It is a time of repair, a time of rest. Life is a constant race. There are short races and there are marathons, but you do not know which race is coming up, so rest and relax. Rejuvenate your body so that you are ready when it is time for the next race.

Do you get anxious when things are peaceful and calm in your life? Do you allow yourself to relax, or do you strive to find something that will add stress and worry back into your life?

Day 364

THEATER/PLAY

Part of surrendering is knowing and having faith that things are happening behind the scenes. Look at the theater. Many things are going on behind the curtain—actors switching costumes, scenes being changed, and much more. You are in the play, on stage, and I am working behind the scenes with the costumes, lighting, and all of the things that must happen before the next scene. You do not see any of this happening. Does that mean that it is not happening? Of course not. Have faith and trust that I am behind the scenes working in your life. Surrender this part of the play to Me while you are on stage in the present. Does the actor on the stage worry or concern himself with what happened in the scene before or what is going to happen in the next scene? No. That actor is concerned with the present moment!

How has God worked behind the scenes in your life? Are you living in the present on stage, or are you concerning yourself with the past and the future?

CHAPTER 30

The Mosaic

Trusting in Me will create
the glorious mosaic of your life.

There are times when you will get a teaching that has an amazing impact on your life. I received this specific teaching from God, and it is still my favorite teaching. It really moved me to see how God is continually putting the pieces of our lives together. There are times when He is working behind the scenes and is adjusting our lives. He loves us so deeply, and we are truly blessed to have such a loving God. I hope this teaching has as much of an impact on your life as it has had on mine. It is a longer teaching but is well worth the read. God bless!

Day 365

God, it always amazes me how You put all the pieces of the puzzle together.

Yes, My child. Do not be amazed. I have been doing this always. It is just that now you see it. You see all of My interrelationships and the things that have to happen in order to fit the puzzle pieces together to make the beautiful picture. When you look at a mosaic up close, all you see are different pieces of tile of all kinds of shapes and sizes. The artist (Me) puts them together, fitting them according to size, shape, and color. He then adds the cement to permanently put the pieces in place, adjusting them ever so slightly. After the cement hardens, you see many pieces that have been put together without seeming to make much sense.

Then you step back and see a glorious picture of you and Me together in total harmony and beauty! Some pieces didn't make sense when they were first added, but after you take a step back, you can see that the pieces were required to complete the full picture. While the cement slowly hardens in one area, more pieces are being placed in another area. Other tiles are being made and cut and added to the picture. After placement, they need to be tweaked, glued, and cemented. Some pieces take more time to make. In ceramics, some colors are more difficult to make. Red is one of the most difficult to make and it takes longer, just as some pieces of your life take longer. The artist is always working on many different pieces at once. Once all the pieces come together, they are cemented into place.

This is similar to how it is in life. Some pieces take longer to form. Some pieces cannot be placed into the mosaic until other events are finished, but in the end, all of the pieces are cemented together. So sometimes you need to have patience in parts of your life. The Artist might be working on a red tile. Other parts of your life come together easily because there is no need to wait on other sections or pieces. Sometimes things happen quickly, but only the Artist knows which pieces will be placed quickly and which pieces will take more time. Sometimes the Artist is working on areas that can be finished quickly, while at the same time He is waiting for the more difficult pieces to be made. Eventually, all the pieces in one area will come together, and the Artist will work on the next area. A mosaic takes much time and patience to complete, but the Artist has much patience and does not concern Himself with time. It will be finished when it is finished. It cannot be rushed, or mistakes will happen and some pieces will need to be removed. So have patience, My child. The Artist knows what He is doing. Your picture will be completed in His time, not in yours, and the final result will be magnificent. Do not force pieces to be rushed or to be placed too soon—or they will need to be redone. Patience and trust in the Artist is the key to life. Be present and accept the piece that I am working on, knowing that I have a vision for your life and that it will take time to complete. We might be waiting on a red piece of tile to be completed before moving on to the next piece or area of your life. Red pieces cannot be rushed, or the color will not be as brilliant as we need it to be.

Have patience and trust, My child, that our mosaic will be magnificent and glorious. We will look back on this mosaic and see not only the little pieces but also the big pieces; not only the jagged pieces but also the smooth pieces; not only the dull colors but also the brilliant red ones. Then stand back and see that it took all of these pieces to make the glorious picture of your life. Trust the Artist, My child. Trust Me with your life—with your mosaic picture. Trusting in Me will result in the glorious mosaic of your life!

Acknowledgments

I wish to thank all those who have walked with me on this amazing spiritual journey with God.

Emeritus Bishop Richard Hanifen, who has constantly shown me love. Your faith and love for God are truly an inspiration. You were the catalyst that began my amazing journey, for you introduced me to Frannie Rose and One Simple Voice.

Frannie Rose, my spiritual teacher, founder of One Simple Voice (www.onesimplevoice.org), and dear friend who taught me how to hear God's voice and who continues to guide me gently on this amazing journey. I am forever grateful to you and love you dearly.

My loving family:
My husband, Mark Freeman, who has always believed in me and with whom I get to share this faith-filled journey;
My daughter, Alexis Hess, who rode the rough waves with me, never faltering in her love and trust in me as her mother;
And my parents, Larry and Susan Blick, who were my first teachers of God's love. I love all of you.

I also wish to thank John Bevere who introduced me to Esther Fedorkevich of the Fedd Agency.

And a deep thank-you to Esther Fedorkevich, The Fedd Agency, who took a chance on an unknown writer and believed in this book; Tori Thacher, the editor, who oversaw this project and continually directed me in the right direction; Holly Crenshaw, who worked so many hours with me editing; Deryn Pieterse, who designed the cover; Paul Miller the copy editor, as well as the others who aided in this endeavor.

And of course,
To God, my first love. You have made this journey of life incredibly full of joy and love. Your unbounding love for me is humbling. I look forward to dancing with You someday.